A HARD DAY'S WORK

More tales from the Country Matchmaker

Patricia Warren

WINDSOR
PARAGON

First published 2006
by
Hodder & Stoughton
This Large Print edition published 2007
by
BBC Audiobooks Ltd by arrangement with
Hodder & Stoughton

Hardcover ISBN: 978 1 405 61682 9
Softcover   ISBN: 978 1 405 61683 6

British Library Cataloguing in Publication Data available

Printed and bound in Great Britain by
Antony Rowe Ltd., Chippenham, Wiltshire

I wish to dedicate this book to all the wonderful people who come into my life, especially the many hundreds of clients I have met through the Country Bureau, which is now in its twenty-fifth year.

It's been a great privilege to gain their friendship and I've always felt honoured that so many individuals have approached the Country Bureau and shared their innermost thoughts and desires with me. I would particularly like to thank them for allowing me to write about their experiences. Without them, this book could not have been written.

ACKNOWLEDGEMENTS

Jill Tait, who lives in my village, has always been a great support to me, and I'd like to very especially thank her for her encouragement and help.

Helen, my editor at Hodder & Stoughton, is so nice to me and has always been a great help.

I know the children have a difficult time with me when I'm writing, and I appreciate their patience and understanding.

John gives me such good practical support with his unbiased reading of my work, comments and criticism. He says he is a saint for putting up with me—and he probably is.

CONTENTS

CHAPTER ONE

A TIME TO BE BORN AND A TIME TO DIE

The stars were twinkling in the crystal-clear black sky over the farm and a circle of people were skipping in unison on the edge of a field. Some of the men, thick-set and muscular after long years in farming, were even holding hands, and in all honesty it was quite odd to watch blokes who wouldn't normally be seen dead showing the slightest of feminine inclinations dancing fairy-footed steps side by side with their mates. 'Bloody hell, Fred, I never thought I'd hold your rough old hands in the dead of night!' said one to another. But it didn't seem to matter—for in the cold night air clock chimes could be heard coming from the radios of cars parked in the nearby farmyard. The gathering of people stopped laughing and chattering and listened to the count . . . nine, ten, eleven, and when the twelfth bellowed across the field they all started cheering and singing 'Auld Lang Syne'. A light was quickly put to an enormous firework that had been set up some distance away, and as the massive explosion of brilliant white light rushed into the sky the New Year of 2000 was rapturously welcomed in by all of us as we hugged and kissed and shook hands.

Leaving the field with our guests and heading for the warmth of the farmhouse, I passed the old stables that had been converted into my office in 1982 when I started the Farmers and Country Bureau, an introduction agency for people who

1

live and work in the countryside. I looked through the windows at the hundreds of photographs of happily matched couples and thought over all those years of matchmaking. What a wealth of wonderful stories I'd experienced, intertwined with a full-bodied mixture of yearning for love and the intricacies of rural life. They were stories full of all sorts of diverse characters—the complex and enthralling stuff of life.

As we walked into the farmhouse we started talking about what might lie ahead for us all. The mothers among us, of course, thought about the future of their children. For the moment, those children had all gone to the large attic room at the top of some stone steps in the old farm buildings. My own children had always used this place for parties and to be with their friends. Up there they could make as much noise as they wanted that New Year's Eve, and it left us grown-ups more space in the farmhouse.

Everyone refilled their glasses and started to talk about the likely changes in this new millennium—on the whole with great anxiety and trepidation as, being mostly farmers, they knew there would be many challenges ahead. I thought also about the millions of others throughout the world that night who would be wondering what the future would bring, individually and within their families. Suddenly the conversation was stopped in its tracks by a smell of burning. Smoke spiralled up, filling the room, but at first no one could detect where it was coming from. Then someone saw flames and we all realised that my husband's jacket was on fire. John had been standing with his back to a candle and unknowingly set the garment alight. He was lambasted as a 'thick, dozy sod' as we all helped put it out!

The candle was next to the buffet food, and as I looked at it I realised that the big joint of beef and my game casserole were missing. Wherever were they? They couldn't have been eaten up yet—and even if they had, surely someone would have left a few bones? Then I thought I heard a noise from under the table. I looked underneath and there, enjoying a luxurious meal of prime beef and well-hung game, were our two dogs. 'If this is what the year 2000 brings,' I bet they were saying to themselves, 'then what a good millennium so far.' I didn't know whether to laugh or cry. I'd spent a lot of time preparing and cooking, especially as regards the game dish, for which I'd collected, over the preceding weeks, pheasant, venison, hare and duck. I'd hoped my guests would get a sample of my efforts, but reluctantly I had to resign myself to the fact that I couldn't retrieve the food out of the dogs' mouths, wash it off and offer it around. What on earth could I do now? Quickly I remembered the huge wedge of Stilton cheese that John had wanted to be left in the pantry for his own consumption. Well, he'd have to sacrifice this treat. And then I realised I'd got a big pot of beef stew that I'd cooked for New Year's Day, when I'd planned not to do any cooking at all. I concluded that my family would just have to starve in order to save the evening, so I quickly got the stew hot and bubbling while I cut the Stilton and searched for biscuits, grapes and walnuts to complete it all.

Very quickly the spirit of the night overcame most of us and we started to be merry. With a bit of drink you get the different angles on life, don't

3

you? The serious sit down and talk even more seriously, as does Trevor, our local schoolteacher. Whenever he goes to a party, the highlight of his evening is to talk about the end of the world—and he was having a field day as in some quarters Armageddon was expected to happen that Millennium eve. He'd got a little group of people in the corner and was enjoying himself to the hilt. Our local vet sidled up to me and said he'd had enough talk about bloody gloom and wanted to live it up before it was too late. With that he disappeared into the crowd.

The jolly exaggerate their merriment and try to involve everyone in hearty games, going around with balloons and blowing those whistles that make raspberry noises. We had one of those Mr Jolly types at this party, and we all tried to ignore him. There was also an example of the nimble-footed, sprightly old man who feels every woman wishes to dance with him. This one's speciality was the rumba, and he kept showing off his dancing prowess to everyone as he stood in front of his latest victim, offering his hand to dance with her. He reminded me of some species of insect with thin bent legs enticing his next mate.

Towering above our prancing rumba dancer was Samantha, one of our faraway friends whom we don't see often. Although she lives on the other side of the country she can smell the preparations for a celebration several counties away, and therefore never misses a party. When she has drunk enough to remove all her inhibitions she surveys every man present, then stands in the middle of the room and fixes her eyes like a cobra selecting its lunch. She starts to sway her hips from side to side, then quickly revs up to a gyrating motion that any Arabian belly dancer would be proud of. This is coupled by a thrust or two of the lower pelvis in a beckoning fashion towards her prey, which means, 'Come hither.' At this point the victim usually prays to the Almighty to take him up to heaven at that very moment in order to get him out of this situation.

Later that night Samantha fixed her intent on the rumba-dancing insect. With perhaps the hundredth gyrating hip thrust of the evening she lost her balance, put her hand out, caught the eight-foot Christmas tree—and tree and lights, glitter and fairy all came crashing down on top of her. It stopped everyone in their tracks and a hush descended, only broken by a high-pitched cry from underneath: 'Get me out of here!' The tree had enveloped the little old man, and he crawled out from under the debris like a freed rabbit. The tree was pulled back upright and there was Samantha lying flat on her back, legs apart in mid-thrust, open mouth full of glittery balls and tinsel. Everyone said it was the funniest thing they'd seen in a long time, and it was pronounced the highlight of our 2000 New Year's Eve party. It certainly far surpassed the expensive fireworks.

Of course, when the Christmas and New Year celebrations were over we all slipped back easily into our everyday routines. I'm always very happy, as I think most people are, to get back into a routine. What amazed us the next day was that everything was still normal. Planes hadn't crashed, Big Ben was still working and no computers had blown up! I think Trevor, the prophet of doom, was secretly disappointed.

I've been working in the Bureau office long enough to feel at home once I walk in and sit down. My first day back after the Christmas and New Year break is always very full—full, too, of the emotions of life such as loneliness, happiness and hope. In this small office I find myself experiencing the whole of human nature. Most people want to change their life to find that very special person to share their days with. Others cannot wait to tell me that they have got on very well with someone over the holiday period and all is going well. And there are always one or two couples that have become engaged or have started to plan being together fully. With such immense diversity my day at the office is never dull.

In early January I usually receive many new membership forms, and I often allow myself a little chuckle at some of the comments. 'Don't want a rough woman.' 'No brown-headed men'—that certainly eliminates quite a few. 'Only want to meet a lady who is big and strong'—many images of what he expected her to do came to mind.

There are always a huge number of messages left on my answering machine over the long festive period. Some messages after Christmas are very poignant, and my enjoyment of the blissful happiness of one can be wiped away by the excruciating loneliness of another—for instance, 'I've been thinking about joining you for years. This Christmas was so bad, being by myself, that at last I'm asking to come on to your register.' One message that surprised me in the New Year of 2000 was from a lady who, although we have never met, has become a very dear, if geographically distant, friend.

6

We had last spoken about a year earlier, when she reminded me that I'd introduced her to her husband when she was seventy-two years old. She described a wonderful married life with him, then went on, 'I'm letting you know that he died several days ago, but I wanted to thank you for the lovely years we had together.' I was greatly affected by this, and felt so privileged to have been part of their lives. Now, here was a message from Nancy again: 'I know you'll be amazed at me telephoning you, Pat, but over Christmas I was wondering if you would think there was a chance of me meeting another gentleman—someone around my age, of course. I know it might be very difficult to do this, but what do you think? I've been on my own now for a year, and I just feel so lonely.'

Oh dear, there's so much less chance the older you get, I thought to myself. I finished listening to her words and sat quietly for a moment thinking a little, then said to myself, *Well, why not, Pat? Go on, put her details in the register and see what happens.*

After my vast number of messages had been dealt with and the Christmas rush of brochure requests sent out I settled as usual to the ordinary work of getting to know a bit about what people had done over the holiday period. Curiously, it seemed that many of my members were in New Zealand that Christmas. Already I'd been told by seven of them that they'd just come back from there. Some were attending the weddings of friends or family. One lady had just bought a house in South Island. One couple went out to meet her family there before they became engaged, and another couple went out to 'just be together'. They could have all formed their own club!

7

As I finished for lunch and stepped outside my office I was reminded that this was not summer in the Southern Hemisphere but winter in Derbyshire. Every branch of every tree in the group that encircles our house and buildings in a distinct horseshoe shape was frosted brilliant white against the azure sky, and I realised how wonderful the farm can look on a clear January morning after a very sharp frost. I could even hear, like gunshots in the distance, some of the branches breaking off because of their heavy coating of ice. Perhaps winter isn't too bad after all. But let's not be taken in. Winter on a livestock farm means even harder work than usual. For in times of severe frost there is hardly any time left in the day, after thawing out all the water pipes so that the animals have enough water, for the routine jobs of milking, mucking out and feeding. Once we've done everything the pipes will have frozen once more, so we are constantly going back to the beginning to start again.

Within that same day freezing fog can descend, so thick that we cannot see the other side of the farmyard, and seep into every crevice of the thickest of coats. When you are over 1,000 feet above sea level, as we are, it would be a miracle to get through a winter without some really bad days. People living at lower altitudes, especially if they aren't farmers, might look on snowfall with anticipation and glee and think of Christmas card images. But for the livestock farmer it just means extra work.

However, time moves on. Eventually January disappears, and when February comes along we usually start to feel a glimmer of hope. The days are lengthening, and the snowdrops appearing everywhere herald spring. On one particular day in March the spring sun was streaming through the office windows and the effect was wonderfully relaxing. 'Ah, wen yu gets yr first bit o' sun on ya back in t' year, it's a wonder wat it al do,' I've heard many times here in the Peak District.

Then the telephone rang. I settled myself on a chair out of that sunshine and became totally absorbed in the conversation. It was a man named Donald, who said, 'I wanted to let you know what a happy few years I've had with my wife, who you introduced me to. I came to you about twelve years ago, about two years after I was widowed. I never thought that it would work and I'd actually meet, fall in love and marry anyone through the Bureau. But it happened—and, surprisingly, with the first lady you introduced me to. But now I know I don't have so long to live, and I want to put my affairs in order. And I felt so much I wanted to speak with you and thank you for all those happy years we've had together.'

I thanked him for speaking to me and said how much I appreciated his call. It was difficult for me to know how to end the conversation, as it was obvious from what he had said that I wouldn't speak to him again. As I put down the phone unexpected tears appeared in my eyes and rolled down my cheeks, plopping on to the papers on my desk. When they landed and I saw the smudge they made I felt a little cross with myself for being so silly, and pulled myself together.

A moment later I saw John walk past my window. *It must be close to lunchtime*, I thought, and got up from my desk and walked out of the office, across the farmyard and through the back

9

door of the farmhouse. He was sitting on the chair by the door undoing his bootlaces. John is a broad-shouldered man, nearly six feet tall, distinguished by his bushy but stylish trimmed beard, which in recent years has changed from a lovely deep brown to hues of grey. He has a great smile and will one day make a real authentic Father Christmas without any artificial enhancements. I started to tell him that I'd just taken a phone call from a man who had told me that I'd introduced him to his wife twelve years ago and they had been married ever since.

'Bloody hell, Pat, I bet he wants compensation from you for doing a twelve-year stint!' he said, looking up with an earnest, concerned expression that was supposed to convince me of his deepest fears.

I burst into laughter and cried out, 'Oh, you old cynic! The man actually said he'd decided to telephone me to say thank you for the wonderful married life he'd had.' I went on to explain that he had recently been told he had a terminal illness, and that he had wanted to tell me how happy they had been before it was too late.

John listened intently, then, with his typical dry wit, remarked that the knowledge of your own mortality could shock any man into believing the happiness of the married state. He looked at me with a sly grin that made me absolutely certain he didn't mean any of what he was saying.

'Ah! You don't deceive me,' I said. 'You're one of the happiest men I know.'

To which he replied, 'Go on, woman, get in the kitchen where you belong and get me something to eat'—but accompanied this with a glance over his glasses that convinced me he was well and truly teasing and knew he was pushing his luck a little.

With no time to put anything proper together for lunch I went for the good old standby of bread and cheese. I beavered away, finding chutney, pickles, salad and anything and everything that I could put out quickly. Concentrating on what I was doing, I jumped about two feet in the air when without any warning one of our really large cockerels gave the loudest possible cock-a-doodle-doo from behind me. Not used to the door being open, he had strutted his way in to announce at the top of his voice his wish to be in the kitchen. I turned round, shooed him out and away from the door and resumed my quest for a meal.

The kitchen is quite a long room and contains an area for sitting in comfy armchairs, with newspapers strewn about, as well as a pine kitchen table in the centre. My navy blue Rayburn range cooker is constantly on, rumbling away quietly in the background. There is a long oak settle down one side of the room, with a bare limestone wall behind. Lots of chairs are lodged beside the walls for visitors' use. John, at the top of the table, always uses the high-backed carver chair that my father left him, and I always sit on the short Windsor chair his mother gave me when we married. It is low and broad and fits my short stature and broad-beamed frame perfectly. Around the Rayburn are the work units housing the 'business' bits of the kitchen. The ceiling is heavily beamed and not at all uniform, and I keep numerous wicker baskets hanging from the beams. This room is the very liveable, warm hub of our home.

As the morning brought some very acceptable early spring sun, if it were left to me I would go and sit outside on one of our farm benches to enjoy this first really warm day of the year while eating our meal. From our garden you can see no other house or farm. It is so secluded and peaceful—and it is good, as any dairy farmer will tell you, to watch your spring grass grow and know it will quite soon be your silage crop. That silage will feed your livestock for the next winter and be the source of your ability to farm and survive for yet another year. But when I asked John if he would like to sit outside to have lunch he didn't share my enthusiasm.

'I've been moving sheep all morning and I've gone and got myself a bit too hot for that. I could do with cooling down.'

I thought this a bit unusual because moving sheep, when you've got a good sheepdog, shouldn't be that stressful. But anyway I resigned myself to staying in the kitchen to eat.

'How did your new dog work out, then?' I enquired.

'Wonderful, wonderful,' he answered quickly.

'Well, that's good. So it made moving them that much easier.'

'Oh yes, without a doubt,' he said, sitting down and sighing with obvious relief.

I heard Charlie and Richard, who work for us, come in through the back door to wash their hands.

'That bloody super-duper sheepdog,' moaned Richard.

Out of the corner of my eye I caught John looking up and gesturing to Richard to keep quiet.

12

'Oh, sorry,' said Richard. 'I'm always putting my bloomin' feet into it, aren't I?'

'Never mind, Richard. What do you mean?' I demanded.

'All right. You might as well tell her—you've started now,' John grumbled.

'Well, he won't admit it,' said Richard, looking at John, 'because he told us this dog would be so damned good. But it's either the dog or the master who should be getting some bloody lessons.'

'Whatever do you mean, Richard?' I asked in surprise.

'Well, it turns out this wonderful sheepdog is frightened of sheep. It's been hysterical, because the dog's hidden behind John whenever it's come close to the flock. And John's run his socks off—no wonder he's knackered. . . . A sheepdog that's frightened of sheep!' he repeated in disbelief.

'He'll be all right—he just needs time to get used to us all and settle down,' replied John defensively.

'Bloody get used to us,' scoffed Richard. 'He's made up his mind he's having none of this running about all the time and he's going to have an easy life now he's here. He's started as he means to go on.'

At that we all sat down, and everyone apart from John smiled silently at the thought of the comic strip image of this sheepdog hiding behind his master because he was frightened of sheep.

'Would you like a cold drink instead of the usual pot of tea, as it's so warm?' I asked them, trying to change the subject.

'Ah, no. I've always had a cuppa, so I'm not for changing now,' was Charlie's reply.

13

As it was Friday, after lunch my job was to go to the bank and then make up the wages for the men and for my assistants in the Bureau office. That always has to be done by 4 p.m., when the farm worker who started at 6 a.m. finishes work for the day, so that he can be given his pay packet before he leaves. But with a little time to myself after clearing away in the kitchen, I decided to take a long cool drink outside and enjoy the sun by myself for ten minutes.

I found it hard to get that morning's telephone call from Donald out of my mind. Nothing anyone can say will take away the inevitability of death, so we might as well recognise that maybe there is a right time in life for us all. I recalled the familiar lines:

To every thing there is a season
And a time for every purpose under Heaven.
A time to be born and a time to die.
For everything there is a reason.

I would dearly like to be able to change things for this lovely man but I can't, so I feel I have to go with those words and these thoughts.

How lucky those of us are who haven't yet had to come face to face with the inevitability of our life's end. I considered my own day-to-day life and, recognising that I am so much at peace with the world, offered up a silent thank you to whoever is the all-powerful up there, for having been allowed to enjoy such a wonderfully happy life. I thought about the work I had been doing for nearly twenty years: helping others to achieve love and happiness through finding successful relationships and marriages, and dealing with people who are frequently very lonely and just longing for someone special in their lives. I reckon I have the most rewarding job in the world. John and I have two healthy teenage children, Ben and Sarah, who seem to be leading fulfilled lives, and we are lucky enough to live away from the noise and dirt of cities. Here in the beautiful Peak District we can drink in amazing scenery in every direction.

But all this wasn't handed to me on a plate. I wasn't born to farming parents, I had to start the Bureau from nothing, and it took many years of struggle and failure to conceive before we adopted our children. My lifelong hopes and aspirations, however—a life in farming, children and to be a matchmaker—have all come to fruition.

As I closed my eyes I thought about my childhood and considered how some little girls dream of being a doctor striding through the jungle and saving the lives of countless African babies, or of running away with the circus and living the life of a carefree nomad. But I dreamed of being a matchmaker. What a strange ambition at such a young age—but yes, I did. I knew matchmaking was for me, and I always knew that given the chance I'd be good at it. I knew I also wanted to live off the land in peaceful surroundings: in short, to enjoy a farming life with a good husband. The next desire on my list was to have lots of children. Little did I know that this of all my wishes would be the hardest to accomplish.

As I started to nod off, my head jerked and brought me back to reality. Instead of languishing in the sun I needed to be up and doing. Quickly I collected up all the chequebooks and paying in

15

books needed for my trip to the nearest town, Bakewell. Some people would despair at the routine of my life. Every Friday afternoon, as well as the trip to the bank, I pick up six oatcakes from the local butcher's. I get the local papers in the village and have a chat to virtually the same people every week. I fill up the car with petrol and head home. That's what I've been doing every Friday all my married life, which is over twenty years. I do love it, however—it's what village life is made up of, and it keeps most of us sane and content.

I always have to dash back to get tea on the table for John and the men who work for us after 3.30 in the afternoon. Having an early midday meal means that if they are working hard, and through to 6.30, they need a cup of tea and something else to eat in the afternoon. Usually it's the conventional tea stuff—bread, jam, cake, fruit—but that day we had strawberries, given to me as a present the day before by someone who came to the office for an interview. That morning, before the milk went away in the tanker, I went out to the dairy, ladled off a small quantity of cream and left it standing all day to thicken. There would be just enough for that afternoon's tea.

Usually John and the farm worker who's going to do the milking at four o'clock come into the kitchen about half an hour earlier. The other farm worker, who will finish work at 4 p.m., will be doing his last job of the day—getting the cows into the collecting yard of the milking parlour. As anyone with experience of cows will know, they understand more about where they should be than we humans do—but when they want to go where they shouldn't they can be annoying beyond words.

Once the men have had their tea and gone out to milk I can have a little bit of time to myself again, until I have to go and collect the children from the school bus. If you live, like us, on an outlying farm you often have to drive into the village and wait for the bus, unless you are really lucky and the kids are delivered to the end of your farm drive. I've gone down to the village now for what seems like centuries, but in fact it's only about seven years.

I wait in the same spot day after day, and I talk to the same mothers who also wait day after day. You quickly get to know each other, sometimes better than your own family, because in those daily five minutes of waiting there is a constant exchange of thoughts and moods. Most days I wait with Karen, who takes me into another world altogether. She and her husband are a city couple who have spent some years in the country with their children and have now decided to emigrate to Spain. That day in March they had just returned from purchasing their new home facing the sea, with the mountains in the distance and Gibraltar not far away. It sounded wonderful, and in my mind I transported myself to a fantasy world of leisurely ex-pat living. But somehow I don't think that is for me.

Ben and Sarah arrived on the school bus as Karen was telling me all about the preparations for moving to Spain. Bags were thrown in the back and homework projects flung to one side as the children prepared to forget school for the weekend. 'Can't we race Karen up the hill, Mum? Go on, we can go faster than that!' they shouted. And yes, I did have a little race with my good friend: first to the top of the hill—a Derbyshire hill, *my* hill, and I wouldn't exchange it, or any other part of my life, for anything or anywhere else.

CHAPTER TWO

'PLEASE, WAVE YOUR MAGIC WAND'

As well as working in the Bureau and on the farm, I'd been inspired by the stories of the people I'd matched to write a book. It was a joy to think back to all the happy, funny and poignant memories. Writing was proving very rewarding but also hard work, and on one particular morning in spring 2000 I was feeling a bit stuck. I needed some advice—but where should I go? After some thought I decided it would be a good idea to get in touch with a similar author, someone who had written about a country way of life. After doing a little research on the internet I came across an author who lived in Cumbria. I found his telephone number and, worrying what he would think of me—he had written many books and I was only in the middle of my second—took a deep breath and dialled it.

'I can't believe this,' he said in tones of amazement when I introduced myself. I wasn't sure what he meant, and then he went on to explain that only that morning he had decided to telephone me.

Whatever is he on about? I said to myself. *Telephone me, me of all people—why me?*

'Don't you remember me, Mrs Warren?' he said. 'It's Bill. I joined your agency over fourteen years ago, but I didn't have any success. Well, I went away and put all my energies into other things—one of them was to write a series of books. But last

19

week I decided I'd get in touch with you again—and yes, this morning I thought I'd actually do it. Yet here *you* are telephoning *me*—after fourteen years, just when I wanted to speak to you.'

We both laughed at the coincidence. I racked my brains, and eventually I recalled him quite well. Then I explained to Bill what my call was all about, and he was most helpful. We ended the conversation with me promising to send him my usual joining pack. But I had some reservations, I must admit, since, I now remembered why, I hadn't been able to introduce him to anyone all those years ago. The difficulty lay not in him as a person—he was a lovely man, intelligent, full of humour, articulate and interesting—but in the fact that he had a pronounced limp and a bent spine. Sadly, this always seemed to put ladies off. I knew that introductions for Bill wouldn't come along easily this time either, and that I would have quite a task ahead—but I believe everyone should pursue the happiness they deserve no matter how difficult it is to find, and I accepted the fact that I would probably have to work very hard on his behalf.

Four days later I collected the early morning post as usual from our box at the end of the drive, and there was Bill's application form—accompanied, I soon discovered, by a longish letter. He said that he was now in his late forties and found it hard to walk because one of his legs was shorter than the other. He wanted to have a family more than anything in the world, and realised that this would make the search even more difficult. Not only would the lady in question have to accept his disabilities; she would also have to be fairly young. I heaved a large sigh—I was under no illusions about how hard this was going to be.

Back in the office, I typed out his profile as I do for all clients. Basically, it consists of all the facts about a person that a prospective introduction would wish to know. I then clipped it to his application form and filed it in my Bureau register.

After leaving agricultural college, Bill worked as a rep for an agricultural feed company for about ten years, then started to help out at a city farm where they kept some rare breeds, and he specialised in pigs. At first it was just at the weekends, and he proved himself to be very good with the many children who visited. Then he started to get asked to go in for an occasional hour or two in the week if a school party was visiting and the children were doing projects. By this time he had gained considerable experience and within about a year, with grant funding, he was taken on full time and put in charge of the educational side. He devoted a lot of time to the rare-breed pigs and within a few years became something of an expert, showing them far and wide.

It was at about this time that he joined my Bureau; sadly, he eventually decided to come off the register when no one seemed interested in him. His letter explained how this rejection really hurt, but he reckoned that if he couldn't find a wife he would at least accomplish other things, and flung himself into getting a small farm of his own and starting to write about country life.

Yes, his perseverance paid off—after a number of years he set himself up in his own farm and started to get books published. He still visited the city farm and worked there occasionally; the Queen visited on one occasion, mainly to see Bill and the champion pigs. He continued to write, and publish, a book a year on average; but no matter what he accomplished he realised he was getting more and more lonely and wished so much to share his life and farm with a woman he could love. Not long ago he had woken up one morning and convinced himself that maybe the best thing would be to get in touch with me again. 'To my utter disbelief', he wrote, 'you telephoned me before I got round to it—after fourteen years of silence!' It was an inspiring but extremely sad story, and I really wasn't certain I would be able to perform magic and produce a happy ending.

Then with a flash of inspiration I suddenly thought of Sally, who also lived in Cumbria. She was in her late thirties and had never been married. Although she had been on my register for a while, she had never actually met anyone. Introductions had been given, but either the man had thought she was too quiet or she had thought the man wasn't right for her. I'd actually spoken to her about two weeks previously, asking her to put down on paper details of the type of man she wanted to meet and send it to me, and now I reached into her file to re-read her reply.

'Most of all he has to have a sense of humour,' she wrote, 'maybe even be a bit of a tease, but especially I want to meet someone who doesn't like going to discos or nightclubs. He must like a nice, quiet country life and he must want to have children.' She finished the letter by wondering if she was a lost cause, but implored me: 'Please use your magic wand on me!'

I smiled at the magic wand bit—but the other criteria sounded all right for Bill, I thought. His books were full of jokes, so he certainly had a sense of humour. But would she accept a man so much older than her? And, most of all, what would she think about his disabilities? He would only be about the same height as her, too. *I wonder, I just wonder*, I thought, and then, *Well, let's have a go.* I knew they both lived in Cumbria, but it is a rather large county and so I felt I should look on the map. I found, to my delight, that they only lived about seven miles apart. I started to have a really good feeling about this.

I decided to write to Bill that day and enclose Sally's introduction profile. He later told me that as he opened his post that morning he saw there was a letter from me but assumed it was just a routine acknowledgement of his registration form. When he opened it and saw a description of Sally he said he couldn't believe the speed of my response! Then, on reading her description, he convinced himself she wouldn't accept an introduction to him. Her profile seemed too good to be true, he said, and he became totally pessimistic about his chances.

When Bill got back to me and said her profile was 100 per cent perfect I told him that now it was time for him to wish really hard, because I had to approach Sally with his description. I decided this was far too delicate a job to leave to a letter, and it would be best if I spoke to her. Once again there was an amazing coincidence, because Sally said, 'But I was just going to telephone *you*, to see if I'm truly that lost cause.'

I gently started to put the idea of Bill into her

mind, telling her all the good points but balancing it with his age and the other things she would have to take into consideration. She didn't even know where he lived when she said, 'Yes, let's be introduced.' Then I told her how close he was.

'Now if this introduction goes ahead, Sally, I want you to promise me you won't rush out and meet each other. Living so near, as you do, you could meet up on the first evening you talk to each other. But you mustn't! It's so important to get to know each other really well before you meet— even try writing,' I said. *Well, he wouldn't have much trouble doing that, would he?* I thought. Then I went on, 'Writing can be good because sometimes you can discuss things in a letter you would never mention on the phone. And whatever you do, don't text each other. You can't show feelings or emotions in a text message, and I've known it ruin relationships before they've got off the ground.'

So the introduction between Bill and Sally went ahead and a few months later they told me all about it. Bill telephoned her immediately. 'She sounded wonderful,' he said. 'She was too good to be true—kind and considerate and caring.' Sally thought 'he seemed a nice man.' They went on to exchange many letters over the next few weeks. It was Sally who first said, 'Aren't we going to meet?' but Bill wasn't sure.

'No one likes rejection,' he told her. 'I'm so happy talking to you the way we are. I'm just terrified it will go wrong if we meet, and I'll lose you.'

Sally replied instantly, 'But you aren't going to lose me—you aren't.'

Bill then started talking about his physical

appearance, to which Sally responded, 'I know. Pat has told me.'

And so, a few weeks after first being put in touch, Bill arrived at their agreed meeting point. Before he was able even to look at Sally he was greeted by an enormous dog. He said it was obviously a case of 'Love me, love my dog.' Anyway, they went out and couldn't believe how quickly the time flew. They had a cup of tea somewhere nice and before they knew it, it was six o'clock. Bill wondered if they should spend the rest of the evening out, but decided he would be pushing his luck. Sally confided in me later that she would have loved to have stayed out longer with him.

Their next date was a drink at a pub. That went very well, and that evening Sally happened to mention how fed up she was with the front garden of her little cottage. Little did she know that Bill was hatching a plan. The following day, while she was at work, he and a friend set to and transformed her garden with a new path and lawn. It was the most wonderful surprise when she arrived back home that evening. The next morning was spent at a garden centre buying plants, which they put in together that afternoon. By the evening they still did not want to go their separate ways, so they went for a meal in a pub.

The following day Sally telephoned Bill and out of the blue asked him, 'Do you think this relationship is going the same way as I think it's going?' Apparently that was exactly ten days after their first meeting. I asked Sally exactly what she had meant. 'Well, I knew he was the one,' she replied. 'The one for me. I just wanted to be with him.'

Bill replied to her question by saying, 'I just don't want to lose you.' That night when he went to bed, he said, he hoped beyond hope that at last, after thirty or so years of trying to find someone special, he had succeeded.

He knew Sally had never had a proper boyfriend before, and that was one of the reasons he was so cautious. He'd had several serious relationships himself over the last twenty years but none had stood the test of time, and after each break-up he'd gone through several months of depression. However, he had learnt the mechanics of a relationship and knew how it felt to fall in love. He realised that she was possibly not in this position, and would maybe need time to understand her own feelings.

Two weeks after their first meeting Sally was due to go to a seminar at the start of a degree course for which she had been accepted. Bill took her there, waited for her and walked her dog around the grounds—but when she came back to him she said point blank, 'That's not for me. I know what I want in life now.' They stood in the beautiful grounds under a weeping willow tree, with spring flowers spread around their feet. As they looked into each other's eyes Sally said, 'I want to be your wife, Bill, and have your children.' For so many years Bill had yearned for someone he loved to say this to him. His heart soared with happiness, and he told me that from that moment his life took on a completely different meaning.

I visited Bill and Sally later on in the spring. Each year I do a couple of tours of the country, planning a circular itinerary that enables me to

26

visit as many successful couples as I can. Sometimes I journey into Wales, sometimes into the southern counties; it just depends on where the latest happy couples live.

When I arrived at Bill's farm it was clear that he had worked very hard to acquire the stock and buildings and the lovely new house. It was also obvious that he was a meticulous man, because everything was set out beautifully with immense smooth lawns around a large ornamental lake and a vast paved area with stone figures—not at all typical of most farms.

I was immediately invited into the sitting room and greeted warmly. Bill was just how I thought he would be, Sally possibly a little quieter. We sat down, me in an armchair and Bill and Sally together on the settee. Bill reminded me that when I first wrote to him about Sally, by return of post, he was staggered to see that I had found someone for him to consider so quickly. I'd put in that letter to him that 'I've got a good feeling about this introduction, and Sally is a very special person.' I admitted to him now that I thought it was going to be extremely difficult to find any introduction for him, let alone a successful one, given the experience of his membership all those years before. But when I had put Sally's form side by side with his, I told him, I had had a good feeling about it.

They looked at each other, then said they would be getting married later in the year but before winter set in—they hadn't announced it to friends and family yet, and wanted me to be the first to know. Bill told me they had decided to have the ceremony in the little church in the village and the reception back at the farm, in a marquee by the side of the lake. He had met Sally's parents, and everyone had got on well. They had also been out with each other's friends. I suppose they were just at that pleasurable stage of knowing absolutely their own destinies: they had both got what they had longed for and wanted for years.

'I never thought it would happen to me. I'm getting older, and it just seemed that everyone could be happy but me,' said Sally.

'We're living as man and wife now,' Bill proudly announced, 'and if we start a baby just before the wedding—well, so be it, time isn't on our side.'

'What are you planning to do after the wedding, Sally?' I asked. 'What about your job and your house?'

'I'll sell my house,' she said, 'and I'm giving up work. I want to be a housewife and mother. We've decided to expand the farm and I'll take over the rearing of the pigs. Bill wants to keep showing his pigs, but with me in charge of the litters that will give him time to do other things around the farm.'

'Maybe I'll even be able to call my latest book *A Family at Last*,' Bill said, at which we all laughed.

As I headed for the door I was shown pictures of Bill with the Queen and his beloved pigs, together with many trophies demonstrating his success. Then a large bouquet of flowers was thrust into my hand and I was given a huge hug before walking out to my car. 'Thanks for waving your magic wand over both of us!' they shouted as I drove away.

CHAPTER THREE

ONE LOVE IN YOUR LIFE

Springtime, for me, is the best season of the year. It always feels exciting that a new year is beginning, and I'm sure this feeling is true for most people. I get up with great enthusiasm once the dreary, dark winter mornings are left behind and I have a definite spring in my step, delighted to be up and doing in the early morning sunshine.

There are three seats in different parts of Lathkill village, which is about a mile away from the farm. If the sun is shining when I am driving through the village I usually see two or three people just sitting on one of the village benches enjoying the warmth. I always like to stop and chat, even if only for a few minutes. Very often it is a group of some of the older men of the parish, now retired, who are putting the world to rights. Stopping and joining them means I have to be prepared to take their banter, so I expect to be teased mercilessly about anything odd that John or I have done recently. But listening to them always teaches me something about the locality, particularly in years gone by.

Some of the characters whom the older men talk about seem amazing. I'm sure they embellish the details every time they tell a tale about the endurance, strength and sometimes sheer stupidity of some of the long-gone inhabitants of the village. We've all heard the one about the man who, for a bet in the local pub, caught and killed a rat with his teeth in front of all the locals. It seems to get more unbelievable each time I hear it. Then there are the stories of the long hours and gruelling toil that farmers endured in the old days. We've been told of one farmer in the 1930s who had dairy cows, but the only grazing land he had was a long way from his house. This, of course, was long before the days of tractors and trailers, let alone 4x4s, and he was only a poor hill farmer anyway. So twice a day, for six miles each trip, he used to carry two full milk churns on a yoke around his neck.

Brian, one of the villagers, told me of the courage of one farm worker in the 1950s who accidentally chopped off his finger, but just wrapped up the end in a bandage and continued working. He never visited a doctor and just let it mend on its own. And what strength that man must have had! When this heroic figure was walking through the village one day, he casually lifted up the front end of a car and held it aloft while someone mended a puncture. After this last piece from the repertoire Percy added, 'But for brute strength there's no one like John Warren—he has to lift up and carry his own wallet every day!'

At other times these old locals will talk over what's happening in their everyday lives, mixed in with a bit of gossip and a lot of joking and laughs. But it's good just to sit there and enjoy the peace of the place and prettiness of the village and not be in a constant rush—to while away a few moments with someone whose friendship you appreciate.

In our area there are quite a number of farming marriages that have broken down, and I would assume that it's the same in most parts of the country. It's just that when people are local and you know them, even slightly, it feels particularly sad. Jim, a farmer living no more than two miles away, was in this position but resisted coming to me for several years. He kept saying to everyone who encouraged him to do so, 'No, I'll meet someone myself. Leave me alone—I'll meet someone.' I knew several local farmers' wives were constantly harassing him to come to me—they told me so. They wanted me to approach him myself, but I never would—people really have to feel the need themselves.

Five years went by and many women had come—and gone—in his life. Eventually he did telephone me: I had to smile to myself that it had taken so long. I asked him if he would like to come and see me.

'No, no, no, I couldn't do that,' he insisted.

'But you only live two miles away,' I replied.

'Yes, but I couldn't bear anyone to see me—neighbours or anyone who would recognise me.'

'All right, I understand,' I said, and started to put his details on the register. Quite soon I thought I knew who would be the best introduction for him. Anne was a reasonably local lady, living about ten miles away. She asked me to her cottage one afternoon for a cup of tea, and I spoke about Jim.

'Oh! No, no—he's too old for me,' she said firmly.

In the course of the next year she had other introductions and Jim met about three other ladies through me. None worked for either of them. So I approached Anne again.

'Go on, just meet Jim,' I urged. 'I really think you're compatible, even though there's an age difference. I can't get it out of my mind that you're

31

so well-matched.'

'All right, I will—though I can't believe I'd get on with someone ten years older than me, so I don't give it much hope,' she said finally.

Jim and Anne were introduced and they met up one evening for a drink. The next day I had a phone call from Anne. 'He's really nice and we got on very well. I suppose I'm surprised—I didn't think we would. I really enjoyed being with him!'

One week after that she asked me to visit her again, and that day I saw an Anne that I hardly recognised. Her whole face was alight; she was excited, bewildered, amazed. 'I can't believe it— it's only a week but he's come here every evening. He's wonderful, and I'm sure we've fallen in love. Why didn't I take your advice and meet him a year ago? Jim says we could have saved a year of messing around—but at least we're with each other now.'

Three months afterwards Anne moved in with Jim at his farm and her cottage was sold. Six months later they had a small wedding in the local church. And no one was more pleased than me that they had found happiness—with a little help from their friendly local matchmaker.

One of the first questions I'm usually asked when people phone up to enquire about the Bureau is 'How long have you run the agency?' Well, I started planning it in the autumn of 1981. By the following spring I had thought how I would do the matching of couples and the administration. I borrowed £50 from the farm account to pay for my brochures to be printed, and to this day John still jokingly reminds me that I've never paid it back.

I can remember the look on the printer's face when I showed him my first brochure design and a mock-up of my first registration form. He was an old man who had probably never come across the concept of a marriage bureau, so he couldn't grasp the idea at all. I posted some copy for an advertisement to the *Farmer's Guardian* newspaper. When I telephoned their office they said they would have to think about it, as they had never accepted an advert like this before. I then approached the *Farmer's Weekly*, only to be told they wouldn't accept such 'personal' advertising. Was I an escort agency, they asked . . . or even worse? But to my great relief, after two weeks of consideration the *Farmer's Guardian* accepted my advert. All this seems so quaint and odd today when you see all the (highly) personal ads appearing in papers and magazines.

Before anyone joined the Bureau I conducted several trial runs on matching people up. Would their education be the most important factor? Background? Type of work? Age? I decided that I would have to take location and age into account before anything else. Then would come the finer points such as personality, physical type, education, style and type of life, and wishes for the future. Of course there were no computers then, so my basic office equipment consisted of a phone, a typewriter and some carbon paper.

I crossed my fingers on the Friday of the first week of May 1982, for that was the day my advert came out. At lunchtime on the Sunday I had my first phone enquiry. Could they have a brochure? And over the following week I received lots more enquiries. In early June people started sending in

33

their registration forms and joining the Bureau.

All new businesses need a bit of luck, and mine came in the way the new members joined. They could all have been of one sex, for instance. Or I could have had a situation where no age group was represented in both sexes, which would distinctly reduce the chance of a match. This wasn't the case, however, as I had a good mixed bag of clients. Very quickly I was able to match people up, write to them about each other and complete my first introductions. I couldn't really believe that I was at last fulfilling my long-held childhood dream. In some ways it felt wonderful to be doing what I had always wanted, but, as with everything that you have waited a long time for, I thought the bubble would surely burst. Luckily, it didn't.

One Wednesday evening in that spring of 2000 I was working late, printing some brochures. Just as I was leaving, at about 9.30 p.m., Iris called—a lovely girl in her early forties with a very kind and sincere nature. Sadly, and surprisingly, she had never been married because she had never met someone who thought she was special. I'd known her for about a year since she had come on to the register and had grown very fond of her. She lived locally and worked as a nurse in Derby, which meant she had quite a long daily drive before she even started work, which some days was at 6 a.m., so on those days she had to be up at 4.30. I had visited her at home and she had come to the farmhouse to talk over the introductions I'd given her. She had now become a good friend whom John and I cared about a great deal.

Iris was very animal-orientated and was utterly soft with all the animals found on a farm like ours, from wild little kittens to the huge beef bull. John constantly made fun of her protectiveness towards them, saying things like he was just going off to drown the last batch of kittens that had been born that morning. I knew he was not going to do anything of the sort, but Iris would take the bait and the mutual teasing was ceaseless.

When Iris and I talked on that Wednesday evening she was all of a fluster. 'I can't believe it, Pat,' she said breathlessly. 'This latest introduction, Mark, is so nice. Actually I didn't want to report in to you too soon, because when I first met him two weeks ago I wasn't certain what I thought about him. But now I've met him three times in all, and our ways and personalities seem to mix so well. I think he likes me as well, because he does most of the travelling—all the way up here from Oxfordshire. I realised—at our last meeting particularly—that he's gentle and kind and sensitive. I know that's right for my personality, and he wants to take me out on Saturday night to Buxton Opera House. So I feel I should invite him to pick me up from my house beforehand, and of course I want to invite him in.'

This seemed like great news, I thought. But Iris was worried.

'I've got to work all day tomorrow,' she went on, 'and I've only just arrived home from a long day today. Friday I'm working again until late. I feel as if the whole relationship will fail if I can't get to clean and tidy my house. I've phoned up all the cleaning agencies but they're busy. Whatever will I do?'

I sympathised. 'I understand—of course you want your house to be spick and span for this

35

special visitor. Well, there's nothing for it, Iris—I'll come and clean your house tomorrow morning. I'll do what I can until about four o'clock in the afternoon.'

There was a stunned silence. 'You would do that for me?' she said at last.

'Yes, I'd do it for anyone I felt deserved some help. I'll be there in the morning as close to ten as I can.'

'But Pat, I've not phoned you up expecting you to do that. I was just going to ask if you knew of anyone I could get to come round at a moment's notice—you know, a cleaner.'

'That's all right, Iris, I know you didn't. And I'm afraid I don't know of anyone else who'd be able to do it. My offer still stands.'

With that she realised it was too good to turn down, and we discussed the location of the key. All next day I dusted, vacuumed, tidied and polished from top to bottom—I'd not worked so hard, even on my own home, for a long time. I was pleased with what I'd done and set off for home at 4 p.m., in time to pick up the children from the school bus at 4.30. I hoped so much that Iris would make a good impression upon Mark and that the date in Buxton would go well.

A day after the event Iris phoned with an update. Apparently Mark's visit to her house had gone very well and she said he had seemed suitably impressed. She said she would let me know if their relationship continued to develop, and promised to keep the house tidy so that another visit from me would not be required!

Thankfully, May that year brought some lovely weather and a hint that summer was just around the corner. In late spring the fields are always lush with grass, and the early morning birdsong which greets you as you walk through the trees takes my breath away. To breathe in the beginning of the new day with its distinctive freshness and watch the sun slowly creeping above the horizon must surely invigorate anyone.

Every May in our small village we have a week of traditional Derbyshire well dressing; culminating in a village market-cum-fete. The well dressing is hard work: we spend a whole week making a very large picture out of flower petals, to be exhibited in the middle of the village in front of the old well. Apparently this custom goes back to pagan times. It died out, but was revived in the last century. Some of the larger villages make four, five or even six pictures, which means they need forty to fifty people or more working every day and every evening for at least a week. In our village the population is only large enough for us to make a single picture. I do enjoy it, although in some ways I can understand how people might say, 'Hasn't this woman got something better to do than pull flowers apart and stick them together to make a picture?' But isn't it good occasionally to do something completely illogical?

The well dressing arrangements begin when specially constructed wooden boards, which have been kept for years by the village, are brought out and soaked in the sheep wash in the nearby river for about three weeks. They are then lifted out by a party of men, usually on a Sunday morning, to be placed on bales of straw in the children's playground. The group of men trundle down the dale that leads to the river.

'Bloody hell, John! Don't go and get yourself drowned in the river, cus you needn't think I'm going to give you the soddin' kiss of life!' was one comment I heard from the distant river bank. So for about an hour grown men play and paddle about in the river, weighing the boards down with stones and putting the world to rights with their banter and chatter.

On this particular May morning we were suddenly told to be quiet by one of our working party.

'Can you see what I can see?' he said. 'Look what's taking place—and they think no one can see them.'

We all watched in astonishment as a well-known lady from the next village appeared on the path that joins the two villages along the river bank. Her brisk pace slowed, and then all of a sudden a van appeared as if from nowhere at breakneck speed, and amazingly with its back doors wide open. She whipped round to the back of the van as it momentarily stopped by the pathway, and quick as a flash climbed into the back and hung on for dear life as she closed the doors from inside.

'Well I never! Did you see who that was?' the mutterings began. 'Ah! An illicit romantic rendezvous on a Sunday morning between a married lady of one village and an inhabitant of another. Then the couples will meet up tonight and think no one is the wiser.' We all laughed at the subterfuge we'd witnessed, feeling like kids who had found some hidden sweets.

But back to the job in hand. It's quite easy to put the boards in the river. But pulling them out is a different matter as they weigh so much more after several weeks of soaking. However, with great good humour the task is always achieved. As soon as the boards are brought back into the village they are stacked on straw bales and then we put a thick layer of clay on top. The clay comes from a piece of local land called Custard Fields. The strange name, I'm told, derives from the appearance of the fields in question, which look just as if a layer of custard has been poured over them.

The actual picture is designed by someone in the village and then it is up to the well dressing ladies, of whom I am normally one, to execute it from leaves, or natural materials such as rock chipping, but mostly from flower petals. Traditionally the picture has been anything that we have felt was appropriate—either a local subject, like the picturesque river flowing at the bottom of the village, or perhaps a local character like old Mr Stone, whose family have farmed in and around this area for many years. One year's picture showed this nice old man standing by his gate, which opens directly into the village square, with his sheepdog at his side and two of the youngest occupants of the parish playing behind him in the field. I feel that including Mr Stone in this scene was a way of recognising the contribution his family have made to our village. His sister regularly does flower arrangements for the church, he and his son farm the land, and his grandsons play in the square. They must be so proud, as a family, to see each new generation make its way in the same locality.

Well dressing week begins in a very relaxed way as we all stand or sit around the picture doing our little part and catch up on each other's lives over the past year. Some women actually give up work for a week to do it—it's relaxing, and takes you back to the days when people would have to pool their efforts to get village projects completed. Margaret usually puts herself in charge of supplying the workers with tea, coffee and cakes throughout the day—it's never a prearranged thing but just happens, and she usually say it's her contribution. Margaret has lived in the village for forty years and was formerly married to a village man who sadly died very early in their marriage. People like her contribute so much to the whole community.

Newcomers to the village are forewarned that their services at the well dressing would be greatly appreciated, and that they should present themselves with one or two little sharp sticks (old manicure sets are good to bring along) and a pair of scissors. They are advised to attach the scissors to their person with a safety pin and some string, or the scissors will quickly disappear. I should adhere to my own advice but I never do, as every year I lose my scissors. What a funny sight we would look lined up—a group of women armed with safety pins and string and sharp implements!

New people are usually quite apprehensive and start their little area tentatively, constantly asking if what they are doing is all right. 'Oh, yes, yes, yes, dear, it's beautiful,' you say, but invariably with really new people you have to patch it up when they have gone, hoping they won't notice. But usually by the end of the week they have become quite skilled and can do as good a piece of work as anyone. I always tell anyone new to remember the words 'It wasn't me.' Someone will always ask,

'Who did that?', and 'It wasn't me' is the phrase most handy to have on the tip of your tongue. It gets you out of any situation.

By the time Friday comes the pace has quickened up in order to get finished by the end of the evening. Someone goes and gets fish and chips for us all, but there's no time to stop and incredibly no one wants to. Backache is ignored, fatigue is brushed away, and with amazing team spirit we all pull together. The cheer goes up when the final petal is inserted: usually the newest or the youngest person who has been helping is asked to do this. The wine comes out no matter what the time—usually around midnight but sometimes it can be as late as 2 a.m.

The men then take over to clean the surrounding wood and paint the boards white. Every woman is dropping with tiredness but satisfied that the job is complete. In that week of well dressing I confess I don't do any Bureau work. I leave it all to my assistant and then catch up with everything on the Saturday morning. It's extraordinary what can take place in the lives of all these Bureau members in just one week.

On the Saturday of that Whitsun weekend, I settled myself in my office and started to open my post. It consisted of new registration forms and reply slips from members to whom I had sent details of a match, asking them to consider the person and then let me know how they feel. Some telephone and leave a message, others fill in the reply slip.

With a first introduction the new member is asked to send a cheque to cover their introduction fees. This is payable only when the member

41

receives their first profile and accepts that introduction. So, with luck, most days I will receive several cheques, which of course are essential to pay for my advertising, stationery, electricity, telephone and wages.

General letters received are always replied to immediately, some by phone but most by post. I always prefer to talk to people rather than write a letter, but even in these days of mobile phones individuals can still be hard to get hold of. So, instead of spending hours phoning around and leaving many messages but not getting anywhere, I turn to the post.

On this particular Saturday morning I picked up the phone when it rang and the voice at the other end introduced himself as Paul from Lancashire. 'I'd love to meet the lady whose details you sent me,' he said, 'but I have a problem that's only come to light very recently.'

I listened intently, for he was a new member and I didn't know too much about him.

He went on to say, 'Before I joined your agency I actually travelled to the Far East in the hope of meeting a bride. I wasn't impressed by anyone I met and came home early, determined that I wouldn't go through with that idea. Anyway, the most dreadful thing has happened. I was notified last week that I was married to one of the girls I met out there, and official papers have been sent to me. Apparently she expects me to arrange for her to come over here and support her. It's a complete mess, and I just don't know what to do. I can't recall going with this girl to any ceremony— let alone a marriage—but my solicitor says the documents look quite authentic.'

I was flabbergasted. 'You *must* have gone through a marriage ceremony,' I said. 'Did you get drunk . . . or can you remember maybe being drugged?' I'd never heard anything like this before.

'No, no, no,' he kept repeating. He finished by admitting he'd got himself, one way or another, into a 'right bloody mess'.

I agreed, and said I thought it would take a while to sort it all out and that I would take him off the register. *That was a close shave*, I thought. At least he had had the guts to tell me.

Back to the post. I opened another envelope and scanned another registration form. Once again, I felt, success would be very difficult to achieve. The client was a man of sixty named Edward, who had never been married and who, judging by his photo, had not been blessed with good looks. To be honest, he was ugly. He had disproportionate facial features and was very short, with a heavy build. I was thankful that he was at least aware of his physical shortcomings. 'By my photograph you will see that I'm not good-looking at all,' he'd written, and continued, 'Can't do anything about it—we all have to accept what we are given.' *Yes, he's right about this*, I thought, and I respected him so much for saying that. I started to type out his profile ready to put in the register, but I couldn't stop thinking how tricky this one was likely to be.

Shortness is always a severe disadvantage to any man. Women just don't wish to be introduced to men shorter than themselves, and most women insist on a man considerably taller than them. So a man of around five foot four immediately has diminished chances: no lady over five foot two would be interested in him, which cuts out a lot of females. Combine this with the fact that he had never married, which would make most ladies ask straightaway, 'Why not?', and the problem of his unattractive appearance, and I certainly had my task cut out here. But I didn't want to be overwhelmed by a negative attitude so I decided to telephone Edward. Immediately I was impressed by the warmth of his tone and how very nice he seemed to be.

'Ah! Me farm's only small, I suppose,' he started to say, 'but it's a grand little place here in Suffolk.'

I went on to ask him if he had ever had a girlfriend.

'No, I've not. Sad, isn't it, for a bloke of my age? I'm a bit ashamed of it, really, and come me sixtieth birthday I was determined to change that. I've also done something else I've not done before. I've recently bought a holiday home in the south of France, and I intend to retire there.'

Wow, this is unexpected, I thought.

Then he continued, 'But I do want to meet someone who would be a country woman but who would like to live part of the time in France.'

'I see,' I said, and thought, *This gets more complicated than ever*.

Then he revealed that he had never even been abroad and had got a friend to buy this villa. Alarm bells sounded, but Edward seemed very confident about it all. I finished the call, having got a good impression of him. He was obviously a man who wanted to change—and good for him for having the courage. So many people don't. He was a pleasant and caring man who had just let life pass him by. Now, in his sixties, he wanted to grasp eagerly all that life could give him. He wanted to find love and companionship and a new life abroad.

I looked through my register and discovered Mary's file. She was a lady who lived in a village not far from Peterborough and had been on my register a long, long while. She had never had any real success—most of her introductions saw her once only. I had been told by one or two of those men that she was quite masculine, and I knew she had spent most of her life as a farm worker in East Anglia. She had been married but it had ended in divorce, and all in all I felt she had had a tough life. She added in her description that she never had holidays and had never been abroad.

Quite a lot of similarities between Edward and Mary seemed to stand out—but then what would he think of her masculinity and what would she think of his appearance? Location was all right, age OK. Both had had working lives in farming, but she had been married and he had not. I decided to go ahead, so completed the proposed match and sent it off to both of them.

After its beginnings in May 2000 the continuing story of Edward and Mary was really lovely to hear in the forthcoming months. They met very quickly and fell totally in love straightaway. After only a short while she moved in with him, and I was told they were planning their future retirement life together in both England and France.

Edward said, 'We're just like a couple of teenagers—we can't bear to be apart and cuddle constantly on the sofa. I just can't believe it would happen to me.' But then he added, 'Doesn't everyone deserve one love in their life?'

Yes, I thought. *Of course they do.*

It's been a long time since I started the Bureau in 1982, and sometimes I wonder how on earth I could have been doing the same job for all these years. To my mind, anyone who does the same work day after day must find it quite dull. My work, however, I have to stress, is not in the least bit dull or repetitive. Every day I speak to different people, with different views, problems and hopes. Every day when I enter the office and sit down at my desk I don't know what I will have to cope with, what challenges will come my way—and, of course, most of all, what great satisfaction I may achieve through matching a particular couple and seeing a successful outcome.

I feel that helping others to meet a life partner and change their life for the good is a very worthwhile service to be providing. I treat it seriously and respectfully, and try to carry out my job to the very highest standards—even though many people regard a job as matchmaker as anything but serious. But I realise I'm experimenting with people's lives and, crucially, their innermost emotions. So I constantly remember this and keep in mind the fact that whatever I suggest can affect their whole lives.

CHAPTER FOUR

MR SUCCESS STORY

Once a year, on the day the well dressing is erected, we have a market in the village square, as do so many small communities throughout the countryside. The event draws hundreds of people and when the stalls open masses of them seem to appear from nowhere. Every year bargain-stalking ladies alight from the bus that comes to the village at noon to make sure they are the first to view the bric-à-brac and jumble. They come armed with several carrier bags which rapidly get filled. Then they walk to the village hall to enjoy the value-for-money sandwiches, cakes and tea prepared by the local ladies—having done the teas for so long they operate with military precision. The stalking bag ladies then go back to the hub of activity to sit for at least an hour on the village benches and view the scene until the raffle is drawn. The late afternoon bus arrives and off they go, to return in exactly one year's time.

In years gone by Lady Caroline, who lived at the big house, was in charge of 'Nearly New'. Every year she would produce a mountain of beautiful, flamboyant hats she'd begged off her well-heeled lady friends for us all to try on and wonder whenever we lowly creatures would wear such creations. This aristocratic lady was determined to get every last penny for village funds, and after watching her techniques of persuasion any Cockney market stall holder would take her on immediately.

The big draw of the afternoon is always the cake stall, with its huge array of home-made baking. All these goodies are made by local ladies in the preceding days. I have a confession to make: I can't bake a cake to save my life. Thankfully, over the years the women of the village who organise all of this have got to know me well. They know I can be relied upon to do almost anything in my community, from refuse collection to organising a really good social event for five hundred, but they know I cannot make cakes for love or money. If they do ask me to do so, I am filled with trepidation for days. Yes, just as the lady in *Calendar Girls* was found out, I will now admit that sometimes I have bought a cake, adjusted it a little to make it look home-made, and presented it with brazen audacity. That's why I have never attended a Women's Institute meeting. Whatever would I do when I was asked to bake a cake?

John is always assigned to the bookstall and over the years various people have volunteered to be his assistant, but their skills never seem to be put to the test because most of them spend all afternoon reading the interesting books that they come across. I'm asked to do the bouncy castle and I cannot understand why this should be so. Why am I not allowed to mix with the adults? My lot is the company of snotty-nosed little kids who constantly ask, 'How much another go?'

Usually the event raises about £2000 for the village hall. By the evening we are all absolutely knackered and those who have helped to organise it all have a barbecue party. Most years it doesn't end until the small hours, and the evening is full of fun and antics. The ladies always have a go on the bouncy castle—have you ever seen about ten fully grown women of various sizes try and bounce up and down in unison? Of course, since I am a large lady the most amusing scene comes when I bounce down and everyone else is flung up into the heavens. We all end up screaming with laughter.

About midnight, as people start to drift off home, someone usually invites the rest to come in 'for coffee', but what this invitation actually means is 'a drop of brandy or a wee dram'. All the bottles are brought out, and after a further convivial hour or so the real challenge comes when those who don't live in the village have to walk home. Those who live in our direction all walk home together, helping each other. This year, we had to leave one parishioner laid out in his cabbage patch, talking quite fluently to the vegetables. Another neighbour who lives about a mile away asked me to point him in the direction of his farmhouse from our drive. Off he went, climbing over walls and greeting cattle as he struck out for home in the dead of night with no light. How he got there I shall never know.

Everyone who has taken part in the money-raising event is invited to the home of our local military top brass, our very own retired brigadier-general, for drinks the following morning, which fortunately is a Sunday. I have to admit that after the revelry of the previous night I can usually only face orange juice. I also tend to suggest to the family that we should support the ladies who serve lunches to the tourists in the village hall. In fact I insist we go there that day for our lunch—at least that gets me out of one job that day.

Very quickly after such a busy weekend we are back to our normal routines. Before we know it, spring has rolled into summer and there is a lush growth of grass all over our fields. Most mornings throughout the warm summer months I stroll (I cannot call it a walk) around the house or down the drive for the sheer pleasure of seeing it all.

The farmhouse is some two hundred years old—not in fact very ancient when you consider that many of the farmhouses in the locality are twice that age. Detached from the other farm buildings, it stands on one side of the farmyard and looks a very typical Derbyshire cottage with its two windows on the front with a door in the centre, elevated slightly from the yard by a flight of old stone steps. Shrubs grow beneath the windows. Years ago, when the cows trailed through the farmyard to be milked in the shed, we would never have been able to grow flowers because they would have been devoured en route. However, times have changed and the cows now enter a modern milking parlour away from the yard.

We have several meres around the farm. These are dewponds which were formerly used to collect rainwater, as a lot of farms on this high limestone plateau had no mains water until the 1950s. The meres provided the only water supply for both livestock and humans. Meres are completely round and drop quickly to about six feet in depth. The main one for our farm was directly at the back of the farmhouse, virtually at the door of the old dairy. When it became redundant it was filled in, and now consists of a circle of concrete surrounded by a border of flowering shrubs. The children loved riding their bikes round and round and round it when they were younger. We do still have several other meres scattered across the fields which act as water sources for the cattle, but all the farms nowadays also have mains water . . .

That July, on the last day before the children's long summer holidays, I was taking my usual early-morning stroll. The children, I knew, were so pleased to be having six weeks off school—did I feel the same at their age? I must have done, though it all seems so long ago now. They had both arrived at that interesting age when they were beginning to consider that their dad and I knew nothing about the world, and they knew it all!

Ben was then coming up for sixteen and thought he was twenty-six. He's tall and lithe, and has black hair with a dark complexion. He has a great smile, laughs a lot and has always got on well with people. Sarah is two years younger, and, as with so many teenage girls today, seemed to be a woman on reaching ten. Quieter than Ben, beautiful, petite and feminine, like him she has black hair, but much longer. She is not so dark in complexion as her brother and just looks as if she has a perfect tan. Yes, they do look quite different from John and me, since as well as being adopted, they have Latin American origins.

We tried to have a baby for quite a while and after a few years decided that, although we enjoyed the 'trying', we'd had enough of the stress of infertility. We adopted Ben first, when he was a few weeks old, and went on to adopt Sarah two years later, at five months. John often says that if we'd produced our own we would never have had two so attractive.

Later that day, as I waited to pick them up from

51

the school bus, they threw their school bags aside with an absolute determination not to pick them up ever again—but of course even the long summer holidays are always over in the blink of an eye. Ben, at sixteen, wasn't sure if he would actually be going back—he disliked school very much and had always liked his freedom. Sarah, not yet of school-leaving age, would of course be going back.

Soon enough it was 6.30 and John came in after finishing milking. After a long, refreshing drink he was off again, this time to check the walls of the new fields the cows would be moved into in the next few days. All the fields on our farm are surrounded by dry stone walls, and gaps occur from time to time through winter frost or the activities of wildlife and even the cows themselves. Dry stone walling is quite an art, and it takes years of experience to do it well. Part of our routine spring work consists of repairing the gaps that have appeared over the winter, and Harold does most of this: he has been our waller for a quarter of a century. But since March and April smaller gaps might well have appeared, and these need to be constantly checked.

When the children were younger we would all accompany John in the evening if he was checking the walls. Sarah would usually ride her pony, while Ben would take the quad bike and show off his expertise. Now that the children were older and didn't want to trail along with two old fogeys we had all started to do our own things on a nice summer evening. While John was occupied in the fields I would very often have a walk with my two dogs down the farm drive. I suppose you could say they walk me, because they have never had leads on their collars and can take this journey any time of the day or night that they wish, as they are always allowed to run free. But it sounds good if I say, 'I took my dogs for a walk.'

If you look over to the east, you can see Lathkill Dale and Bradford Dale. In the distance limestone walls skirt rocky outcrops, with big areas of woodland and smaller clumps of trees dotted around. There are specks of black and brown contentedly chewing their cud, and the whole landscape is dotted with grazing sheep. This southern part of the Peak District is so beautiful, with the undulating peaks and dales and the swathes of different green hues from the woodland. If there is a pretty sunset, as there was that evening, it seems there is no nicer part of the world to live in.

But at last everyone heads home. John returned that evening from his walling, Sarah from grooming her pony—called Magic because he is totally black—and Ben from seeing his mates in the village. When John got into the house he was chuckling to himself.

'Whatever's the matter?' I asked.

'I was laughing because tonight I found a packed lunch in the stone wall I was mending. I remembered a while back Harold coming into the house and asking if I could give him a sandwich. He said he knew he'd brought his "pack-up" to work and thought he'd put it on the wall till later. Then, when he wanted it, he turned round and it was missing, and he couldn't understand where it had gone. Silly bugger! Of course he couldn't find it—he must have put stones all round it and done

53

such a good job he couldn't even see it when he'd finished the wall.'

Which just goes to show what a good job Harold does for us. Neither livestock nor sandwiches stray from fields where *he's* been walling.

Saturday morning began sunny and bright, just like the day before, and John, as usual, was up at 4.30 on the dot to start getting the cows in from the fields. In recent years he had started to use the quad bike, but for thirty years before that he always did the job on foot. The cows were spread out over the fields but he never had to spend time getting every single one to the milking parlour—all he ever needed to round up was enough to start milking, the rest always followed on their own, and when Charlie or Richard arrived at 6 a.m. they straightaway made sure every cow was lined up in the collecting yard outside the parlour doors. Charlie had been working for us on the farm for over fifteen years and was our mainstay. Other farm workers had come and gone, but Charlie knew us, our children and the farm like the back of his hand.

When Ben was about four years old he was playing one day alongside Charlie in one of the barns. He gave him quite a lot of cheek and, quick as a flash, Charlie took off his big leather belt and pretended that he'd tan his backside with it for such a 'mouthful'. Ben took fright and ran as quick as his little legs could take him back to the house, where he scurried up to his room. I was none the wiser until I realised that Ben had been in his room most of the morning. When I investigated I made him apologise to Charlie when he came in for his next meal. Since then Charlie has always laughed

54

at the speed with which little Ben ran away from him that day and they have been the best of mates, with Charlie receiving the utmost respect from Ben.

Richard worked for us for about eight years, right from leaving school, until he took the plunge and started up his own business. I used to look out for him considerably in his early years with us. He had no mother and I suppose I tried to take on that role. If the other farm workers were teasing him and he told me about it I would stride out to the farmyard, virtually with my rolling pin in my hand, to defend Richard.

When Ben was about nine he had a Jack Russell terrier who was, lo and behold, called Jack. His favourite pastime was catching rabbits. Towards dusk one autumn day Ben came into the kitchen and asked if I'd seen Jack, because he himself hadn't clapped eyes on him since getting home from school. I said he was probably up in the wood at the back of the farm trying to catch an owl in the twilight—nothing seemed to daunt that little dog! But as it got darker he still didn't appear for his dinner and, although we went all round the farm calling for him, he didn't come home. Ben, beside himself with worry, got up several times in the night and came downstairs to the farmyard to shout for him.

Next day Ben was too upset to go to school—I let him stay at home because I knew he wouldn't concentrate anyway. He searched high and low all day, roaming the fields and calling, 'Jack, where are you Jack?' By teatime I really feared the worst and was getting ready to help Ben face up to the loss of his best mate when Timmy, our other dog,

55

all of a sudden pricked up his ears, barked in a very positive way and set off up the back fields at a trot. 'Follow him quick,' I commanded, and both children ran after him. I went to find John, who had just finished milking. We could see Ben climbing the second gate, with Timmy a good field ahead, still trotting purposefully.

'You follow them and I'll be there in a flash,' John said. Off I went as fast as I could, and when I arrived at the top of the hill, puffing and panting, there was Timmy scratching and pawing the earth round a small hollow in the ground. Ben was on his knees, desperately trying to dig with his hands, hot with running and close to tears. I got down too and tried to pull some grass out of the way, but we couldn't make much progress. Looking round, I could see that it was an area full of rabbit holes. It seemed like an age before John arrived with Richard, who very sensibly was carrying a spade. Ben, Sarah and I stood back while the two men dug and Timmy scratched, until eventually a small brown and white face peeped out, covered in soil, but very much alive and delighted to see us. He wriggled free and Ben scooped him up and threw him in the air for sheer joy, causing much yelping and scattering of soil. I was in tears, so was Ben— and John was close to them as well. But he just scratched his beard and said it was a good job someone like Richard kept calm and remembered to bring something useful when dogs got stuck down rabbit holes. Richard got a lot of kisses and effusive thanks for being the great person he was.

'For that favour it's about time you bought us that new tractor, John,' he said, winking at me. Richard had been trying to persuade John for

56

months that a new tractor was needed. Secretly I knew he'd done all sorts of things to it to try and finish it off, but to no avail. 'I've given that tractor so much grief,' he had complained to me, 'but the bloody thing still won't die.' Here he was, trying another tack. I honestly can't remember if John did relent at that time, but Richard certainly deserved it.

Time marches on, and by the summer of 2000, with the children well into their teens, I had for some years happily left them to their own devices on a Saturday morning. It enabled me to be what I call 'on duty' for that part of the weekend.

So, early on that July Saturday I busied myself around the house for half an hour, tidying up, then washing the kitchen floor on my way out to the office, hoping that no one would walk over it for ten minutes until it dried. I was sure no one would, as John wouldn't be in from milking until 8.30 and the children would certainly have a lie-in today, the first day of the summer break. If I can get an early start in the office and do an hour's work before breakfast I am always very pleased. That day I went to the previous day's unfinished paperwork and two new registration forms presented themselves—by the look of it, I couldn't have had two more dissimilar.

With the first form came a book that the young man told me had been put together by his PR! Well, that *was* unusual—not many farmers have a PR. Rupert's personal card was attached, and as I turned the pages of this large tome with his family crest on the front and back covers I was able to take a look behind the scenes of his everyday life. Yes, it's a one-off to have something like this to look at—but very intriguing, and I wouldn't mock it at all.

There was, first of all, a group photograph of all his family, from mother and father to sisters and their husbands and all their children. Then I came to a family tree with an individual photograph of each member placed above their name. Photographs followed of family life with Rupert, showing him with his nephews and nieces. It was really enchanting. A whole page, describing how the family made their money and listing all their assets, was headed 'The Success Story'. The following pages went on to describe the main farms in the family and the type of farming done, their attributes, and the livestock prizes won. Lastly in this big thick book that seemed to have been put together just for me, Rupert's hobbies and interests were detailed: hiking in the hills, horse riding and skiing. Then his playthings had a photograph each—a classic sports car, an up-to-the-minute Range Rover and a thrilling little kit car. Wow! And right at the end I got to see a photograph of the man in question—tall, handsome, masculine, great smile—straddling stepping stones placed across a river with a staff in his hand as if he was master of all he surveyed, which he possibly was.

I went on to read his registration form: 'a farmer but also entrepreneur in eastern Europe'; he was six feet five with a 'rugby player build'; he 'glows and radiates health' and obtained five A-levels. Then he went on to say he was fluent and communicative, full of fun and laughter, positive and optimistic, with tremendous energy. He was thirty-four years old and had never been married—

too good to be true, but he definitely said he wanted me to find him someone special to settle down with. I dreamed a little and wondered if he would consider someone a little older, well, maybe just more than a little older—but would that really matter? Say someone like me?

I fantasised that every morning we would drive out in his fabulously expensive open-top sports car, over which the sun would shine continuously, to survey the country estate. Later the gardener would come to the house with freshly grown produce that would be given to my cook. Yes, I was now fed up, as most wives and mothers get to be after many years of getting three meals a day seven days a week—I wanted a cook. I dreamed that the cook would produce luscious meals with one tenth of the calories of normal food, so within the blink of an eye I would acquire a sylph-like figure that would be the envy of any supermodel.

After lunch—served by my staff of course—a siesta would be taken—relished, obviously, in the arms of my six-foot-five stud. Then we would motor off for the afternoon, possibly calling at a number of select boutiques to buy a tantalising array of new clothes for me. We would visit new and interesting friends, and most evenings would be spent in a fabulous restaurant. At the end of the day I would once again find myself snuggled up to my man in the largest bed you could imagine.

Right, Pat, you can just forget that, I said to myself as I picked up the next form and realised I had to switch modes instantly. I never usually make comparisons because we are all so individual, but as I read it through I could hardly fail to notice the complete contrast.

'I'm just an ordinary fella,' wrote Bill, 'and I haven't a lot to offer a lady, but I'm fed up with being alone. I rent a small cottage right in the Somerset countryside. There's no electricity, no mains water—but it's beautiful to me. I work around the locality doing odd jobs, anything from hedge laying to ditching and fencing, and I do a lot of tree pruning and apple picking. Just enough to pay my way. I don't have a car and try to be as self-sufficient as I can. Do you think any woman would like to share my life in this beautiful part of the country?'

'Wow, what a difference!' I said out loud to myself. Then I realised that if anyone listened to some of the lengthy conversations I have with myself they would think I belonged in a lunatic asylum. *What a lovely old-fashioned true countryman he seems—no worries about materialism and what the chap down the road has*, I thought. Then I fell to fantasising about a life with him, and visualised myself cooking over his open range fire, bare-footed and wearing my red gingham apron. From the side oven I'd take out towering loaves of freshly baked bread, to be spread with lashings of my home-churned butter and blackberry jam made from the hedgerow.

Oh, yes, I could get into that scene just as much as into Mr Success Story's lifestyle. But I had to work—to type out their two entirely different profiles and put them in the Register. I had just about finished them when I saw it was time to go back into the house and get breakfast ready for the men, who would be coming in at 8.30.

As I entered the house there was noise and confusion. I couldn't quite understand what was going on, and then I saw three sheep running about all over the kitchen. I started shouting, 'Get them out! Get them out!' But the more I shouted the worse things got, because there was no one within earshot to help and in panic they ran first into the hall and then into the sitting room. Realising the impossibility of getting them to march one by one in reverse through the house, I quickly opened the French windows and out they popped, just as if it was their everyday habit to take a stroll through our living quarters.

'Whatever's going on, Mum? called Sarah as she finally responded from upstairs to my cries for help.

'Three sheep in the house,' I replied. 'I suppose I must have left the door open when I went to the office. But then again, they shouldn't have been out of their field.'

'Oh, I see,' she said calmly, as if it was an everyday occurrence to have livestock in the house, then turned round to go back to bed. Then 'Oh, I forgot,' she shrieked, and suddenly started dashing about as it had suddenly dawned on her that she had a suitcase to pack because tomorrow she was going away on holiday with a friend's family for two weeks. But I knew all her clothes were washed and ironed, so putting it all together in the case could be done quickly.

Ben had decided he wanted to accumulate some money so he amazed his dad, when John came in, by asking if he could do a bit of farm work—a rare request, as he had frequently said he definitely didn't want to farm as a career. Work was quickly allocated, and after breakfast we all dispersed to our various tasks: Sarah to get everything ready for her holiday, the men and Ben to work outside, and me to the Bureau office again.

The morning went by quickly. There were many telephone calls because it was a Saturday, and those people who don't find it easy to call on a weekday could do so today. There were a lot of brochure requests, some from people who were quick and business-like and others from people who talked at great length—indeed, told me their whole life story. And, of course, there were clients phoning in to describe how their date had gone, or to tell me they were bringing the introduction to an end.

Iris called to tell me more about the continuing romance between her and Mark after his first visit to her house back in the spring. But she remained apprehensive about its potential for success. It was many years since she had had her last boyfriend, and she feared even to hope that this relationship could go well. Little did she know that Mark had confided in me too, saying he felt exactly the same. They were two people whom I had first got to know well quite independently. Each came to the office for an interview, but it was about a year before I thought of putting them together because I thought the distance of nearly a hundred miles between them was too great. Both had received other introductions, which had not gone well for either. On first being matched they spoke for ages on the phone, so when they did meet they knew each other well, felt very relaxed and—wonderfully—seemed really to like each other. I was optimistic, but felt we would all just have to wait and see.

That particular Saturday I realised I had quite a

lot of 'dating' going on that day. A very young couple I'd put together, both only twenty, were meeting that evening for a drink. They were both quiet, shy and desperate to have, respectively, a boyfriend and girlfriend. 'It's so exciting,' the girl had said to me on the Friday. 'He's spoken to me twice and he's called me "honey"—I can't wait to meet him.' Before I leave the Bureau office on any day I always feel so fortunate to be part of these people's lives. *How could I ever give it all up*? I say to myself.

That afternoon, as I walked over from the office to the house to prepare lunch, I heard something strange in the distance. I stopped walking and listened again.

'Help! Help! Is there anyone there?' The voice wasn't shouting, as you might have expected, just repeating the same words. There was possibly a little more urgency each time, but certainly no raising of the voice.

I walked round the buildings and arrived in the collecting yard leading to the milking parlour. Parked in there was a large tractor, and kneeling on top of the cab roof was Florence, an old lady from the village who occasionally walked up to the farm to have a look at some of the sheep and lambs, which she loved.

'Oh! Thank goodness you've come,' she exclaimed. 'He's there—there, be careful,' she added nervously as she clung to the tractor roof for dear life.

'What do you mean, Flo,' I asked. 'And what are you doing on top of our tractor?'

'It's that bull,' she replied, pointing to our massive Aberdeen Angus, who is really a little sweetie but looks so aggressive to any stranger, as he came snorting round the bottom end of the collecting yard.

'Oh! Flo, I'm so sorry—you must have been very frightened. Midnight wouldn't hurt you—but I suppose you wouldn't know that. I'll just put him back into his pen. He shouldn't have got out, but obviously he has.'

When he saw me he turned round, walked to his pen about twenty yards away, then stood and waited for me to open the gate. Meek as a little lamb he sauntered in, possibly saying to himself how grateful he was to get back to safety after that old lady had frightened him almost to death.

I took Flo over to the house and gave her a cup of tea. She told me she didn't want to shout for help because she thought that might provoke him more. But when she found herself caught in the yard with him she had no option but to climb on top of the tractor.

'How I did that I don't know,' she kept repeating.

'Neither do I,' I kept saying.

I just couldn't keep a straight face as I remembered the sight of Flo, in her seventies, with her long tweed skirt, hat skew-whiff and clutching her handbag, balancing precariously on the tractor roof. From sheep behaving like the proverbial bull in a china shop to a real bull behaving (even if Flo took some convincing) like a pet lamb—and all in one morning. Who'd be a farmer's wife!

CHAPTER FIVE

LOVE IN THE LONG GRASS

Everyone sat around the table for lunch that day, and the children had obviously put their heads together because John and I were immediately pounced upon. They thought it would be a great idea to have a sleep-over for about ten of their friends at the farm that night—they wanted to put the big tent up and all sleep out. 'And why don't you and Dad have a bit of a party as well?' they added hopefully. I guessed immediately what they were after—if the mums and dads were invited, they wouldn't be reluctant to drive Ben and Sarah's friends over here.

John said, 'Well, I don't mind. And it's going to be a warm evening, going by the weather forecast—but I imagine lots of our friends will be doing other things.' It was a bit of a crazy idea, I thought, so impulsive—typical of children, really. But hey! Life is for living, and I've always loved doing impromptu, mad things.

'Well, there's only one way to find out,' I said. 'I'll phone around.' So I called a number of couples, and back came the replies: 'We'd love that' and 'I love spur-of-the-moment parties.' Knowing there might be as many as twenty people, I sat down and announced that everyone would have to muck in. The children said they would put tables and chairs out on the lawn—enough for twenty-four, because you never know who else might turn up. Then I started to think about what we could have to eat.

I'd get a piece of beef out of the freezer and cook it slowly all day. If I cooked two chickens as well they could be turned into a large cold chicken dish by tonight. It was all very predictable and not very exciting food, but I reckon a lot of our friends are quite happy with the old standbys. I'd do rice to go with the chicken and jacket potatoes with the beef. I could make up several salad dishes, and strawberries were still very plentiful in the shops so we could have those as a pud. The barbecue could be lit, and a combination of sausages and beefburgers and bacon rolls could be cooked for the children. We've got two good small local shops which would supply anything I didn't already have in the house. I said I'd go and buy the beer and wine, Sarah was happy to prepare all the strawberries and Ben volunteered to wash all the jacket potatoes. With that I got them both to give me a solemn vow—else their hearts would be slowly cut out by me personally—that they would be back in the house at 6 p.m. to help with laying out the drinks and buffet.

By 8 p.m., when our first friends started to arrive, we had everything ready. About half of those coming would be dairy farmers, so we knew they wouldn't be with us that early. By the time most of them have finished milking, bathed and changed and travelled here, it is usually some time after eight.

The evening was still lovely and warm, so I reckoned we would be able to do it all outside. The chickens had cooled down and been made into Coronation Chicken, with apricots in a curry-flavoured sauce, and the rice had been cooked. A

66

large salad had been prepared to go with the beef, and the barbecue lit. I'd put a notice by the side to suggest that people cooked things for themselves. I personally hate barbies from the host's point of view—because if you take charge of it yourself it means you spend the evening cooking instead of talking to your friends. There was wine and cold beer and cider and soft drinks for everyone also to help themselves to.

Everyone said they thought the sudden idea to have a summer party when we knew we were in for some hot settled weather was really great. Ben and Sarah piled the gear needed for camping out into the pick-up after the children had had their food, and about eight friends jumped in the back before Ben drove off. Although not yet seventeen, he had been driving vehicles around the farm for many years, and as long as he was on private ground it was perfectly legal. He drove up over the fields to their favourite spot which overlooks a prehistoric stone circle called Arbor Low; it's also close to a wood, which would give them a good supply of firewood from dead branches. We have farmed the ground on which Arbor Low stands for many years. Erected about four thousand years ago, the stones have long since fallen to the ground, but the mounds going round the stones still form a complete circle.

Meanwhile we adults ate, drank, talked and all in all had a really good evening. It seemed no time at all before we realised someone had got to drive up the fields to bring down those children who weren't staying the night. 'Let's all go up,' it was suggested, and without much more persuasion three 4x4s were fetched and off we went.

Usually when you go up the fields at night it's to finish off last-minute haymaking or silaging, or to bring down a cow which is calving unexpectedly. Without such arduous tasks to contemplate, for once it seemed quite a hilarious spree speeding across the fields. Once there, we all decided to take the night air by the stones. Now I know you are thinking that we all became drugged with wild-child enthusiasm and danced naked around this pre-Christian site. No, I'm sorry but we didn't do that—even though it was suggested by some of the men with the bravado that men tend to exude when there's a pack of them. We women joked about what the men would do if we actually said we were game for it, because we all knew that if we'd called their bluff (or buff) they'd probably have run a mile.

In fact we just sat on the mound in a line and looked at the wonderful panoramic view, from Buxton in one direction to Leek on the other side and Ashbourne in the south. The night sky was crystal-clear, and the whole expanse of earth and sky transfixed us. There was an atmosphere that was hard to describe, perhaps to do with the mystery of this piece of land that had known humankind for so long and yet had always remained remote and isolated.

My mind went back to the days when Sheffield University were doing an archaeological survey, and asked us to let them know when we were ploughing near by so that they could come and search for artefacts. Before they took everything they found back to the university they came and put it all on our kitchen table. It was awesome to see in front of me spearheads and flint axes just picked up from the soil, and as all the professionals seemed to be wearing rubber gloves I realised, as I gently lifted the objects off the table, that I was the first person to hold them since a man in the Bronze Age made, used and then probably dropped them.

With a shriek from the kids we all came to our senses and went over to the tent and the small fire the children had made. All the girls were returning home that night with their parents, which I was pleased about—the last thing I wanted after such an enjoyable evening was to have to be on patrol preventing boys and girls from indulging in any improper behaviour. That just left four boys up there.

I have to admit I'm hopeless at washing up and tidying away late at night after I've had people to the house. I'll put food away, of course, but I cannot abide spoiling a nice evening by starting on housewifely tasks last thing. I like to depart to my bed genial and carefree, with a few glasses of red wine mellowing my mood and letting me drift off to a peaceful and contented sleep. Anyway, I willingly got up at six the next morning (John had been up and gone a good hour before) to do all the washing up—still in my nightie. When it was all cleared away and we were back to normal I went upstairs and showered, and pretended as I came down the stairs that a wonderful fairy had come into my kitchen and cleared everything away. I do this quite often, and it's a very happy feeling.

At breakfast that morning we had a lot of people round the table. The four boys who had camped overnight appeared, then John and Richard came in, and so with Sarah and myself we made nine. As I was cooking the food on my Rayburn, with the early morning sun streaming through the kitchen window and the sight of John outside watering his flowers, I suddenly felt what a very nice comfortable image this was. It was an image of farm life and family that I'd always wanted to experience from the time when I was a little girl dreaming about my future life. I thought back to my early years in industrial Redditch in Worcestershire. My parents didn't love the outdoors as I did, but my father's father, Grandfather Victor, was a farmer, and from as far back as I could remember I went to stay at his small farm in the rolling green Worcestershire countryside between Stratford-upon-Avon and Worcester. I always knew that I wanted to live and work on a farm, possibly quite an isolated one, with my future husband and children. And here I was today, stopping for a few seconds to appreciate how my dream had come true and was all around me.

Breakfast went well, and amazingly nothing got burnt—as it so often does. The boys disappeared when a dad arrived to take them all back to their respective homes. Ben went off to answer the telephone and then unexpectedly announced that he had to have some good clothes as he was going to church that morning. John and I nearly fainted on the spot! He went on to explain that he would be attending a christening with his girlfriend's family (just arranged on the phone) and therefore needed his suit. We nodded to each other quite proudly—he was the one, wasn't he, who at the age of twelve refused to go to the village church 'ever again'. Now here he was, voluntarily dressing up for church today. Miracles do happen!

'Can't find my trousers, Mum—you'll have to find them for me.' I inwardly confirmed to myself that my little boy, even though sixteen, couldn't do without his mother.

I walked upstairs and found Ben rooting around in John's shirt drawer. He pulled out a cream one and promptly stated that although it was nicely folded in the drawer, it really needed ironing.

'I'll do that now for you,' I said.

'Oh, no,' he replied. 'Kristy will iron it for me.'

So it wasn't true after all. I wasn't needed as a mum—my job had been taken over and I was redundant.

John's reaction, when I sat down at the kitchen table again to drink my coffee and told him, was, 'Good God, woman, you should be pleased that we've been successful in rearing him and your duties are quickly declining. If he doesn't need you as an ironing mum any more you should be glad about it.'

'Well, yes, if you put it that way,' I said, still not over-convinced.

Off Ben went, suit and shirt over his arm, when his girlfriend's grandfather, Don, came to collect him.

Next I turned my attention to Sarah. Today was the day she was going on holiday with her friend's family to North Africa, so I asked her what she had packed and then started reeling off a list.

'Got that, Mum . . . yes, got that . . . yes, and that . . . I made a list like you do, and everything's been taken care of,' she insisted.

Her friend's father appeared to pick her up. He was early, and I was worried that Sarah might not be ready.

'Oh, yes, I am,' she said.

'But I'm sure you need my travelling experience to be able to pack for your first holiday without us,' I cried.

'I really have got everything, Mum,' she countered. Everything truly has been taken care of—I remembered how you do everything when you pack.'

John winked at me and smiled. 'There you are,' he said, when Sarah had gone to fetch her last bag. 'You've obviously raised her successfully as well—you've made her independent. Be grateful. That's what we do all our parenting for—just for days like this. Then when it all turns out right you seem to want to convince yourself we're *not* successful.' He was right, of course. She seemed so sure of herself, and I'd just got to accept that both our children were growing up fast.

Five minutes later we waved her on her way. John and I turned to each other and realised that we were by ourselves until Ben returned home after his christening party that evening. This was a rare occurrence, as there always seemed to be someone else with us in the farmhouse, be it family, workforce or visitors.

It was turning out to be one of those magnificent summer days. I drove down into the village, and everyone I passed waved at me. I stopped several times to have a few words with people, and returned feeling privileged to live in such a lovely community.

The afternoon was marked by baking hot sun, but with a little breeze that just kept it perfect. John and I decided to walk through the eight acres of land we had recently bought. He said he wanted to do a bit of wall building, as there were a few sections that had deteriorated. It was a piece of land we had wanted to purchase for many years, and now, to our great pride and after considerable negotiation, it was ours. The views were stunning, and as we stood and looked over the valley we could see the immense stately home of Chatsworth in the distance.

Our walk started with John picking up the occasional stone and placing it in the appropriate place on the wall, but then we decided to sit down and feel the sun on our faces with the soft breeze wafting up from the valley. Sitting down in the long grass on a hot summer's day seems to lull any couple, no matter how old, into romance and love making, and before long we were like teenagers. With the wild flowers around us, we lay and watched the skylarks soar over our heads—and after our love in the long grass, we both knew that we had found our paradise.

CHAPTER SIX

MEMORIES

As I strolled back home and walked into the farmhouse I knew that the happiness we all strive for, day in and day out, was something that I had actually found and was all around me. But isn't it difficult to recognise it when we have it all, and bewildering when we have to accept that the striving can now finish? I went to my favourite spot just outside the French windows overlooking the front fields. Unusually, I was the only person on the farm that Sunday afternoon, and it was so quiet that I easily drifted into reminiscing about those early years when John and I first met.

I was living and working in Staffordshire at the time and, having a day off, I decided to attend a local farm sale as there were quite a lot of farmhouse effects to buy. I looked around but, as sometimes happens at auctions, the catalogue exaggerated the quality of the items and I couldn't get interested in anything. My car was parked quite a long way off in one of the far fields, and I was walking back through the farmyard towards it, when suddenly the heavens opened. But I was lucky enough to be able to duck for cover in a nearby shed.

As I dived in I glimpsed a man who was also sheltering from the downpour. We spoke, of course, of the dreadful weather, and gazed out at the rain which was deafening as it beat down on the corrugated roof. The roof was also leaking quite extensively, so even though we were under cover we were still getting rather wet. His flat cap was pulled right down and his collar turned up, and I think I had the hood of my wax jacket over my head, So we couldn't really see much of each other. We started to discuss the auction—just small talk, and nothing personal, to while away the time.

Then he asked me where I was working, and a bit about myself. I had trained as a nurse after leaving school, and was working for an agency that sent me all over the country looking after people. He said he lived near Bakewell in Derbyshire and very often came over to this part of Staffordshire as he'd been brought up in the locality and knew it well. I told him I'd never been to Bakewell but understood it to be a lovely market town.

'Come over,' he said. 'Let's meet up and I'll show you around.' He asked for my telephone number so we could arrange a meeting, and as he finished writing the number on his sale catalogue I looked up into his face for the first time. His coat collar fell aside and revealed a bushy brown beard! I've always adored a beard on a man, the bushier the better. I was instantly transfixed, a shiver shot down my spine and I wondered what on earth was happening. Here, in the middle of the Staffordshire Moors, in a muddy wet cowshed, I had bumped into the image of my romantic adolescent dreams.

John contacted me a few days later and suggested he drive out to where I was and we'd have a drink at a local pub (I had thought we were to meet for him to show me Bakewell, but never mind.) Now I had the opportunity to look at him properly for the first time, as I hadn't paid that much attention or indeed been able to see him that clearly in the dingy shed. He was tallish, with a kind, appealing smile and a mass of brown curly hair. His glasses added character to his roundish face, he was broad and masculine—and he still had that fantastic beard!

We had a really lovely evening together, and when it was time to go our separate ways John asked if he could see me again. I was delighted—a dairy farmer who made my stomach turn somersaults, and maybe I fell in love with him and his beard that very day. I was about to suggest we met up the following Saturday, perhaps for a picnic, when he said, 'Of course, I'll have to get the hay in before I can see you again, so it may be a week or two, depending on the weather. I hope you don't mind.' Well, what could I say?

Every evening he would telephone me after haymaking, and through those calls, although we had only gone out together once, we got to know each other well. Then, quite unexpectedly, I had to go back down to my parents in Worcestershire, and even though he had by then finished his haymaking we couldn't easily meet up. 'Never mind,' he said, 'I'll write to you', and with that we started to write virtually every day. His letters were to the point, pleasant but not sentimental. However, we found we could put down on paper so many things that we wouldn't have considered talking about on the phone, and really got to know each other well. He told me he thought my first letter was 'so beautiful': compliments mean such a lot in life.

After a week or two I was able to tell him that I'd accepted another job 'up north' with my agency, this time in the countryside between

Sheffield and Barnsley. His immediate reaction was that on my first day in Yorkshire he would come up and we'd go out again. But I became increasingly reluctant and frightened, a response which I couldn't understand at all. Then I realised the reason was that because we seemed to get on so well on the phone, I was dreading the thought that, when we actually started to meet up again, we might *not* get on so well and this relationship might fail.

He didn't tell me about this until later, but for our second date he gave a great demonstration of what I was to come to recognise as his characteristic thoroughness. Concerned that he might not be able to find the pub where we had arranged to meet, the previous evening he had done a trial run. So on the evening that mattered, the journey held no problems for him. It was a lovely summer evening, and this time we walked for a while before ending up again at the village pub. We talked and talked, and he repeated his invitation to come to Bakewell so he could show me the town and his farm. The evening ended in a very lingering kiss.

Unfortunately, everything went wrong on the Sunday morning when I was supposed to be meeting him in Bakewell. The worst was that I ran out of petrol and ended up one and a half hours late. I realised then that this was a very special man, because he had certainly not given up on me and was still waiting on Bakewell Bridge at 12.30 when I should have been there at 11 a.m.

A little way into our lunch, at the Cavendish Hotel in Baslow, John held my hand across the table and said he wanted to ask me if I would marry him. I was astounded—had I heard right? This was only the third time we had met. Very kindly I explained that, although I loved being in his company and felt fond of him, it was ludicrous for two people to consider marriage so soon.

Lunch over, he took me to Chatsworth. As we walked round the gardens I discovered he was a very persistent man, as once again he asked me to consider marrying him. It was a beautiful afternoon and I nearly succumbed. But not quite. 'No, no, no—now stop doing this. To consider such a thing is ridiculous,' was my reply.

At around 3 p.m. it was time for John to return to the farm to milk. He had said he'd like to take me back there, and he'd told his parents he'd be bringing a lady home that Sunday afternoon. Off we went in John's car (I'd left mine in Bakewell), and there was John's father sitting in a large upright wooden chair next to the fire in the main living room—the fire, I learned, was always lit in the big black-leaded grate even at the height of summer. He was wearing a bright white shirt that had obviously been freshly put on for that afternoon. John's mother had clearly changed too, into a flowery dress, and the table was laid for afternoon tea which they always had at 3.30 so that milking could begin at 4 p.m. I liked them both straightaway, and felt comfortable with them. Lashings of strawberries were on offer, picked fresh from the garden. Then quite quickly I found I had been left with Mother while the men went back to work. A slight inquisition took place, but a not too harsh one. I could tell what a great sense of humour and understanding of life John's mother had and liked her so much immediately.

When John got back after milking in the heat of that July afternoon he stripped off his work shirt, and as he passed me in the doorway on his way to change upstairs he brushed close to me. For the first time, I smelt his masculinity and knew for certain that there was something quite special between us.

That evening we went out to a concert for which John had bought tickets. What a lovely day it had been—how happy I felt with John, and how much at ease with his parents. In the interval we found a quiet spot and he promptly told me that he never gave up on anything he wanted. Once again he said, 'Will you marry me?' And once again I protested that it was impossible to give him a proper reply having only known him such a short time.

John persisted. 'I don't need to know you any longer—I know you're the wife I want. Why waste time? I'm not the sort of man to be too flowery in my words over this, but I know I want you and I can't court you over the winter. I'm a livestock farmer and I'll be very busy during those months. If I can't see you, our relationship won't last all that time—not with you far away. Marry me now . . . soon . . . before winter. September will do.'

Before I knew it I was taking a deep breath and saying to myself, *Here comes that leap of faith that sometimes you know you've just got to go with, even though logic says no.* And so I said, 'Yes. Yes, I will marry you.'

With that he kissed me and said, 'Good! Well, that's it settled, then.'

Throughout the rest of the evening I couldn't listen to the music for the pounding in my head that said, *Have you done the right thing? You've only met him three times—how can you promise your life away?* On the journey back to my car John didn't mention his proposal and my acceptance. Was he having second thoughts? I decided I wouldn't say anything because it had been a mad idea. If that was how he wanted things I would go along with it and completely ignore my answer. I was convinced he was regretting it all, or else he'd have surely mentioned the biggest decision that either of us had ever made.

When we got to my car he said, 'Well, what about Wednesday?'

'Wednesday . . . what for?' I asked.

'To get engaged,' he replied.

Shocked to the core, I spluttered, 'Well, I suppose that's all right.' I was absolutely lost for any other words.

He'd obviously decided it was time to find a wife for himself. It was what he'd planned and wanted, and he'd found one before the winter set in. Nothing more, nothing less. We were married in Bakewell on Michaelmas Day, at the end of September, which was two months later.

I smiled to myself, sitting on the patio on this lovely Sunday afternoon, remembering our extremely brief courtship and, since then, the ups and downs that we had gone through. The downs were, I suppose, no more than many marriages go through. Downs that test you out as a couple and in the end either bring you closer together and make that cement even stronger, or cause cracks to appear and weaken your marriage. The worst downs for us were connected with children. I had always desperately wanted to have a family, but

80

had suspected for a while that I was infertile. I told John about it after accepting his proposal but before we became engaged.

'I want you to think about this really seriously,' I said, 'because I think there's a risk I won't be able to have a baby. If it's very important to you to have your own child, then maybe we shouldn't get married. You really have to think about it.'

His reply was, 'Don't worry about it. Let's try to have our own, and if not we'll adopt. I'd like five in all.'

And that was our first down—that I couldn't conceive, and we had to go along the long, plodding road to adoption. Our worst down was the time our first adopted son died, after being with us for two years. We clung to each other through the agonising months afterwards, comforted each other and gradually got through it, thankfully feeling even closer.

Working hard together in our own business and pulling in the same direction have given us some of the best ups. Things like buying land to expand the farm when we've wanted to do it for years, calving a cow together in the middle of the night, or getting through another lambing season. But without a doubt the highest ups were when Ben and Sarah were each placed in our arms after such a struggle to have our family. With the wisdom of hindsight, we decided to forget John's plan for five. And so our wonderful, crazy decision to marry after meeting only three times (and before winter set in) turned out to be a good one.

My reminiscing was brought to a sudden halt when out of the corner of my eye I noticed a car coming up our drive. It seemed we had unexpected

Sunday afternoon visitors. As the car got closer I realised who it was. Pauline and Jim had each come to me about three years before, and about a year after that I'd introduced them. And the reason for their unannounced visit, if I had guessed right, filled me with pride and joy.

Pauline had told me her philosophy had always been this: if you spend a day with someone, even if you don't click you can have a nice day out and part as friends at the end of it. You haven't got to think *Well, this could be the one*. You should take it as a day out—just going out with a friend. But when she met Jim she said, 'This one's different.' She said she felt so comfortable with him because he was warm and reassuring, and quite early in their relationship, they'd decided to live together. 'If you don't do something', she told me, 'you never get anywhere.' She said she thought, *What have I got to lose? A dear friend had just died. I was devastated. Life doesn't go on for ever—go for it.*

Pauline had had some difficult times before meeting Jim. Married in her twenties, she had very much wanted to have children but none came along. IVF had just started, so she had several tries at that but it didn't work. Eventually her marriage broke down, possibly through the stress of not being able to have children. In her second relationship the same scenario took place: infertility, IVF, feeling heartbroken and then the end of the relationship. Several months after going to live with Jim, Pauline said, 'It doesn't look as if we will have children together, and we've got to come to terms with this sad fact. I'm definitely not having IVF now—anyway, at forty-two I'm too old. For twenty years I've been desperately trying to have a child, but I'm going to stop thinking about all that now. The most important thing is that Jim and I are together.'

Just before Christmas I had had the most astounding telephone call from them. Jim spoke first, and said they had some news for me that they could hardly take in themselves. I knew they had got married about six months before, and had gone away for a late honeymoon about a month afterwards. Pauline then came to the phone and told me she had just found out she was pregnant. I must admit there were tears from us both at the incredibility of it and the absolute joy that it would bring into their lives. No one could have failed to be moved.

Pauline explained how in the months after their honeymoon, they thought she had started to go through the menopause—they never dreamed it could be a baby. They even went to Alton Towers when she would have been three months pregnant. 'If I'd known, I would never have gone on all those things, upside down, at great speeds!'

So I had a fair idea why they had turned up at the farm that afternoon. I looked across as they got out of the car, and there in the carrycot was a most beautiful little baby girl. They lifted her out and put her into my arms. Of course I cried a little—any woman would. 'She's just as much made by you as by us,' they insisted. 'Without you, she wouldn't be here now.' And that made me cry a little more.

Later, after this gloriously happy little family had gone, I suddenly remembered I'd promised to take John a drink. I thought he would be very hot, walling all this time in the direct sunshine on our new eight acres—especially after the exertions of a few hours ago! So I put ice cubes in the flask with stone-cold water and orange juice and off I went. As I searched around the wall where I expected to find him he wasn't to be seen. Then I looked over towards the nearby trees, and as I walked in that direction caught sight of him fast asleep in the shade of a wild cherry tree, snoring to his heart's content. With his straw hat tilted to cover his face, he looked at complete peace with the world. I felt he deserved a break, given the constant hard work he did. Very soon we would be silaging again. It was always a tough job with long hours, so a bit of extra rest now wouldn't hurt him. I went to put the cold flask by his side, but he heard me and woke up.

'Ah, it was grand to have a bit of shade when I sat under the tree. Then I seemed to somehow lean against the trunk, and as I was looking over towards the dale I just fell fast asleep.'

'Ah! What a blissful life you've got, Mr Warren,' I promptly told him.

CHAPTER SEVEN

BABY LOVE

To see and hold and cuddle any of the babies that have come about because I've pinned two pieces of paper together seems to me as much of a miracle as a successful treatment must feel to an IVF doctor. To hold Pauline and Jim's new baby gave me so much joy. Maybe because the getting of our own family was not easy, the production of a baby is even more special to me.

Later that day, when I had peace all around me, I thought about the years during which John and I were desperately trying to make a baby. That conjures up a delightful occupation, doesn't it? But it isn't so really, because of the constant pressure that spoils the enjoyment of it all. When you are an adolescent girl you dream about being with your true love and having all the pleasures that those damn adults have. To turn over in bed and lie in the arms of your beloved any time you wish seems a wonderfully grown-up thing to do. However, once you are actually in that situation, but face difficulties in conceiving, the bedroom scene is not so delightful. You go through many years of turning over to your partner with a thermometer stuck in your mouth, nudging him and saying, 'Come on, get to it—this is a good time.' The romantic dream simply flies out of the window. After several thermometers had worn out and we had grown tired of visiting hospitals, and with no IVF available at that time, John and I decided to adopt.

Our first child was our beautiful little Matthew, who came to us when we adopted him at two and a half years old through our local Social Services. We couldn't adopt a baby because we were told that, at thirty-five years of age, we were too old. Yes, twenty-five years ago society was very different. Couples older than their twenties were considered unsuitable to adopt a young baby.

Our world came apart when our dear little Matthew drowned, in a freak accident, at the age of five and a half. Disbelief and denial were our immediate reactions. But you have to face facts and cope with tragedy, and eventually after months of tears and sorrow from both of us we accepted that we were childless once again.

Just before Matthew died we had been approved by Social Services, to adopt a second child, one, as they termed it, 'age appropriate' to Matthew—maybe a year or two younger than him. When we eventually returned to that organisation and asked to be considered again for a young child, they told us that as we were by now in our late thirties, in their opinion we should have a much older child. This we did not want. We had not gone through any baby stages, and so desperately wanted to nurture and bring up a baby or very young child. We let things lie for a little while, as there just seemed to be no solution.

Then, one Sunday afternoon as I was listening to the radio, I heard about a couple who had had just the same difficulties as us. They were talking about how they had adopted their family from a third world country. I'd never considered that at all, but now I thought, *Why not? We could do that*.

86

If other people can do it, so can we. The interviewer continued to stress how difficult it was, but equally that if you had patience and willpower you could build your family from young babies who desperately needed a home. With no Social Services in most third world countries, you could argue that these children needed help even more than those in Britain. In the UK, although poverty and neglect do exist, instances where a child dies of starvation or has no one to look after them are rare, and tend to make shocked headlines. But in third world countries many babies are born who may well not survive childhood, and even if they do, destitution and a terrifying life on the streets is all that their future holds.

I couldn't wait until John came in from milking to tell him what I'd heard. Could we think about it?

'There's a lot to consider,' he replied, 'but I don't see why we couldn't look into it.'

After that conversation we did a lot of research, and eventually we decided to write to thirty-three different embassies, countries and orphanages all over the world. We got each letter translated into the appropriate language, then they were all posted on the same day at the local post office. I remember sitting on a seat in the village after I'd done this, looking at little children as they walked by with their mothers and wondering if what I'd just done would ever bring us our family.

We had a positive reply from just one of those letters. We very quickly visited the appropriate embassy in London, made up our minds and flung ourselves into the task of getting together all the necessary paperwork.

First we had to apply to Social Services for them to give us the social report they had previously compiled on us and for it to be updated. They didn't know if they could do that, they replied. They would have to consult their senior managers—no one had asked for this document to be sent abroad before. In due course we heard from them again: no, they wouldn't do that.

Our reply was, 'Right, we'll get a report from a private agency who would use an independent social worker.' To which they then responded, 'All right, we'll let you have it and update it for you.' Great! We were on our way.

But we still had a long way to go. Psychological reports on us both had to be obtained, and the interviews for that took weeks to arrange. Then we needed medicals, a report from our accountant, a banker's reference and bank statements, even a document from the National Farmers' Union. Our vicar gave us a good reference and three couples supplied testimonials. In total we had over twenty documents which all had to be translated, notarised by a lawyer, authenticated by the embassy and then sent to the authorities dealing with the matter in Central America.

The day we sent them off, by special courier from London, we were convinced nothing would come of it. But, about two months later, we were telephoned by the translator we had used, who said an important call was due to come through for us the next day. We were to be at her house at midday. John and I were sure it was to tell us our paperwork had not been accepted, or something equally negative.

The translator stood there with the phone in her

hand and translated for us, phrase by phrase: 'We have a healthy four-week-old baby boy for you. He is big and beautiful, and we would like you to be here in one week to start processing the paperwork through our courts for you to obtain guardianship of him. You can bring him home a week after that when he is six weeks old.'

It was unbelievable! At last we would be having a tiny little baby of our own. We couldn't take it in. We laughed, we cried, we hugged each other, we hugged the translator—we would have hugged anyone at that moment. We went home quite stunned, but quickly woke up to the reality of having to get ourselves to a remote part of Central America within a week, along with everything we would need to look after a baby. But of course we did it—nothing in the world would have stopped us. One week afterwards the most beautiful, gorgeous, adorable little baby boy in the world was handed to us, and we named him Benjamin John.

The formal adoption of Benjamin would be completed in the UK, but not until he had been with us a year. Then we had all our paperwork updated, translated, notarised and authenticated once again, and sent it off to Central America.

Two years later, after we had asked to adopt a second child, another telephone call came through to say they had a little girl one week old waiting for us. Once again we were told we couldn't bring the baby home until she was six weeks old, but then things started to go wrong with the paperwork abroad and it was several months before we could collect our daughter. Those months of waiting were horrendous: she was waiting for us, she had no one to love her, but she couldn't be ours until an appointment for the adoption hearing had been obtained in the courts.

We had a big shock when we first saw our new little daughter. She was not big and healthy as Ben had been, but yellow and thin with sunken eyes. The people who had been looking after her had apparently only fed her rice water. Her skin was loose, and instead of gaining weight she had obviously lost a lot. It was a very difficult situation. Her tummy wasn't used to proper milk, so when I tried to feed her she brought it all up. I really thought she wouldn't survive.

John was far more optimistic than me. He was right: we used patience and very diluted soya milk, and she started to take her food a little better. Once we were home our doctor came to see her straightaway and said he felt she would have died in another two weeks if she hadn't been given better nutrition. Gradually little Sarah Anne, as we named her, started to put weight on. She will always be small, but she is a very bright girl and certainly knows her own mind.

So the pursuit of babies has taken a lot of our energy. Now, all these years later, I try to put something back into the adoption world by sitting on adoption panels, where decisions are made regarding the acceptance of couples who wish to adopt and the matching of children for adoption.

I do make an effort to look my best when I attend a panel. So you can imagine my horror when one of my front teeth fell out shortly before one of these meetings. I couldn't bear to look at the black gaping hole, but even so it took me some time to pluck up the courage to see a dentist. I eventually found one who was very sympathetic and he put in a temporary bridge until I could have it seen to properly. It looked just like normal, and I was so pleased to be able to laugh again and move my mouth when I talked. However, the pleasure was short-lived—the bridge broke and I was toothless once more. The dentist couldn't fit me in for ages, so I just had to manage.

To get round the social problems, I devised a plan. If I was seeing someone whom I didn't know very well, I wedged the tooth back in the gap and didn't talk much. My good friends soon knew who they were, because I didn't bother putting it in for them. It was a great joke among our friends who saw it as a mark of their standing with me. They felt they had been paid a compliment if I didn't put the front tooth in: 'You feel at ease with us, and that's good.' So of course I was relentlessly teased when I did put it in: 'Oh! Trying to make a good impression, are we?'

I was soon paid a compliment myself, when I was made chairperson of the adoption panel.

Now here I was on the eve of my first meeting in this important role, but still with a black gap in my mouth. There was nothing for it but to wedge the tooth in and hope for the best. I fixed it before I got out of the car, then sailed confidently into the reception area, well briefed and wearing my best black suit. But by the time I got to the door of the committee room my tongue told me that the tooth had gone—I stopped dead. Where had it gone? I looked on the floor. It was nowhere to be seen—I must have swallowed it! I had to face a room full of people expecting me to be articulate and in control, when all I really wanted to do was hide.

After five minutes I decided it didn't really

matter anyway—we had to deal with much more important issues where vanity had no place. But when I got home and John asked, 'How did the toothless wonder get on, then?' I really had to laugh at the situation. In fact the summer of 2000 seemed to be full of curious incidents of this sort— nothing earth-shaking (at least to start with), and mostly funny with hindsight, but I did wonder at the time if my luck was deserting me a little. Here's one of the funnier ones—even if the joke was on me.

I had been into Bakewell one day that August— it was hot, and I vowed I would never shop again when the temperature was so high. Anyway, when I got back to the farm I pulled up inside the gate at the end of the drive, removed the key from the ignition because the same ring held the little key that unlocked the mailbox, and checked the box for post. On my way back to the car I caught the heel of my strappy sandal in the cattle grid and fell, sprawling on the drive and dropping everything. I didn't actually hurt myself, but something much more inconvenient happened—the car keys went through the grid and ended up tantalisingly out of reach in the dried mud at the bottom.

I knelt down to try to fish the keys out with a twig, but the metal bars of the grid were agony and I knew I'd have to think again. Then I remembered that when Ben had dropped his favourite Matchbox toy car down a drain we had hooked it out with a wire coat hanger. Off to the house, then.

I started across the field but soon abandoned my smart shoes as the grass was so uneven. I therefore had to take extra care to avoid cowpats and thistles. The sun was scorching hot on that still afternoon, and by the time I got to the farmhouse I was desperately thirsty. The only cold liquid in the fridge was some Strongbow cider: I poured myself a large glass and gulped it down. Then I hauled myself up the stairs, hoping to find a wire hanger amongst all the others amassed over the years— wooden ones from gentlemen's outfitters, some that had been crocheted by an old aunt, some pretty Laura Ashley covered ones that had seen better days, and of course lots of plastic ones from chain stores. I was daunted when I opened the wardrobe door and saw the huge crush of garments I had to wade through. As I reached into the mass of clothing, a large cream hat trimmed with pink roses fell off the top of the wardrobe. I bent to pick it up, and sat down on the bed to try it on. Then I just fell back on to the bed, overcome with exhaustion and heat—and no doubt the cider too. It was heavenly to lie down, and as a bee buzzed around my thoughts went back to the wedding where I had worn that hat. My eyes gradually closed, and I drifted into a deep sleep . . .

I was roused unceremoniously from my dreams by the sound of loud voices and car horns. I dragged myself awake and, feeling like lead, stared at the sunlight-dappled ceiling. Very gradually it dawned on me that there was a commotion going on somewhere outside.

I stumbled to the window and, peering out, saw to my dismay a great throng around the gate which I had blocked with the car. How long had I been asleep? What was I doing in the bedroom anyway? Then I remembered the lost keys. I yanked all the clothes out of the wardrobe and hurled them around until I found a wire coat hanger. Then I tore downstairs, fumbled my feet into John's wellies which happened to be by the door, and stumbled down the field. Half our herd of cows was around the gate, with very full udders and inquisitive gazes. I pushed a path through them, waving the coat hanger and telling them not to stand there looking so stupid.

As the situation became clearer, I could see that waiting to come in were not only Charlie on the tractor with a trailer, but also the man from the Water Board come to check the reservoir, and John in his best suit just back from a sweltering day on duty at the magistrates' court. The line of vehicles looked a bit like a carnival. I could see John striding towards me and he looked very cross, and I'm afraid to say that at that stage I shoved the coat hanger towards Charlie, muttered something about bloody keys and bloody cattle grids, and walked back once more down the field in as dignified a manner as was possible in wellies five sizes too big. *We all have days that are better than others in life*, I thought.

CHAPTER EIGHT

THEY COME IN THREES

And then the 'curious incidents' began to get slightly more serious. The afternoon in question started like any other. John, Charlie and our new man, Roger, left the house after they'd had their midday meal. We'd taken Roger on a few weeks previously, after Richard had decided he wanted to see a bit more of the world and had gone lorry driving. Roger had a few funny ways—but so do we all, and we decided to take no notice of them.

The men usually came back into the house for some tea before they started milking at four. But I heard the back door bang much earlier than that, and wondered why. Then I heard an almighty shouting from John and saw him run through the house towards the front door: 'Lock the doors! For God's sake, lock the doors!' Whatever did he mean? He just kept repeating it: 'Lock the doors!' And then added, 'Roger's gone mad!'

I rushed towards him demanding to know what was happening.

'He says he's going to kill us all,' shouted John, as he bolted the front door.

Just at that moment there was a tremendous banging on the outside of it accompanied by: 'I'm going to get you and kill you! Come out, you bastard!' I rushed to the window and saw Roger hammering on the door with a huge metal rod, wearing a terrifying expression and literally foaming at the mouth. I jumped back, realising

95

that if he saw me he would break the window.
Then, looking up, I saw Ellis, the contractor who
had brought his little Bob Cat machine that
afternoon to clean out one of the farm buildings,
peering out from behind a window in our first-
floor grain store across the other side of the yard.
Obviously he could see what was going on and had
run up there to get out of the way.

'We'll have to call the police,' John said.

The thought flashed into my head that maybe I
could talk some sense into Roger, so I suggested it
to John.

'Well, go on, but I tried outside and got
nowhere. In fact, it seemed to make matters worse.
Have a go—talk to him through the door.' He
quickly added, 'but you're not going out to him.'

He was right. I couldn't do that—from the look
on Roger's face I think I'd have been battered to
death. So from behind the door I asked Roger to
tell me what the matter was, to which he screamed
back that Charlie had been unfair to him and so he
was going to kill everybody. 'What has Charlie
done?' I asked. At that he seemed to struggle to
remember, then went on to shout incoherent abuse
at John again.

'I'm calling the police,' John insisted. As he had
been a Justice of the Peace for about twelve years
and sat as a magistrate every week, he was calling
on his experience as well as using his common
sense by avoiding violent confrontation. So he
made a 999 call and gave them an accurate account
of the situation. We were told not even to think of
going out and facing Roger.

The shouting and swearing and banging
continued for what seemed an eternity. Sarah, who

was at home as it was still the school holidays, came running down from her room to find out what on earth was happening. I just told her to get back upstairs and lock herself in.

Then all of a sudden Roger shouted that he was going to find Charlie and 'kill the bugger'. That really worried us, as we didn't know where Charlie was or if he even knew what was going on. What would happen if Roger attacked an unsuspecting Charlie from behind? As Roger stalked off, presumably to look for his victim, John started to unlock one of the doors as he felt he must intervene, if only to try to prevent Roger from finding Charlie. Fortunately at that moment two police cars came up the drive with a police van behind. From where Roger was he couldn't see them, and so when six officers and two dogs rushed into the farmyard they were able to surround him immediately and lead him away to their vehicles.

I was shaking with fright—not least because of John's insistence on going out and facing Roger, which had only been forestalled by the timely arrival of the police. Ellis, the cleaning contractor, was similarly affected. Now that things had calmed down he left his hiding-place and came down the stone steps into the yard, still with a big piece of wood in his hand. 'First thing I picked up to defend myself,' he said. 'God, I'm sweating that much even though I've only got me vest on! I've not seen anything like that before.'

The police officer in charge asked us how long it had all been going on, and as I looked at the clock I realised I was due to pick up Ben in the village. A few seconds later a third police car arrived in the yard—and out got our son. Apparently this last vehicle's driver wasn't with the others and hadn't known the way to our farm, and so had asked a local in the village. The local happened to be Ben.

'I live there,' he had replied. To which the policeman had said, 'Well, get in the car and show me the way home!'

Ben, of course, was mystified, and Sarah, who had by now come down from her bedroom, was engrossed with the whole thing. We were glad when we realised our fears for Charlie's safety had probably been unnecessary. 'What the bloody hell has been happening?' he demanded as he came into the yard and saw the heavy police presence. Ellis had apparently shouted to him from up above to hide, but without being able to tell him why. Ellis told us, with a grin on his face, that he wasn't sure if he wanted to come to do contract jobs on our farm again if the stress of working with John made everyone go crazy!

Later, the police explained to us that Roger was obviously under the influence of drugs, and it seemed he also had schizophrenic tendencies. In our naivety it had never occurred to us that this might be the explanation for his occasional quirks of behaviour. Of course, Roger never returned to work for us. I visited his family a few weeks later to return a few possessions he had left at the farm, and discovered that he was having treatment for his substance abuse.

Given the organised, fixed pattern of everyday life at the farm, none of us could quite believe what had taken place that day. We all sat round the kitchen table having a soothing cup of tea, and milking did not start on time that afternoon. Nevertheless, despite the shock and the realisation that events could have turned out very nastily, we were sad that Roger should have had to depart in such a way. Fortunately Richard came back to us a short while later, after his spell of seeing life in the big wide world.

That night, John and I talked over the events of the day as you do when you go to bed. But shortly after I had drifted off into a nice slumber I heard banging on the door again. *Ah, I must be dreaming*, I thought to myself without opening my eyes. The banging continued. *No, no, I must just be imagining it.* I opened my eyes, and this time there was no doubt about it—that was a definite banging on our front door. God! Had Roger come back? Was he wanting to kill us all again? I sat bolt upright.

'John, John, wake up! There's someone banging at the door again.'

'Don't be silly,' said the sleepy voice at my side. 'The police have taken him away and it's two o'clock in the morning.'

Then he listened, and jumped out of bed. We both looked through our bedroom window—and there was a woman in a skimpy evening dress banging with all her might on our door.

'My car's on fire! Please help me! Please wake up and help me!' she was screaming.

I started to run down the stairs, but John stopped me and suggested that maybe she was just saying that to make us unlock the front door. *Gosh, I'd never thought of that.* We opened the window and asked her where her car was.

'On the road,' she replied, and we both ran over to look out of another window from which we knew we could see the road. There on the lane at the end of our drive was a burning car.

'She'd never do that just to make us open our door,' said John.

We both ran down to her and asked if there was anyone trapped in the car, and luckily there wasn't. So 999 was dialled for the second time within twenty-four hours. Ben and Sarah had woken up and enquired sleepily, 'What's going on *now*, Dad?'

The fire brigade came and put out the flames. The police appeared and took a statement from the driver in our kitchen. After cups of tea, they took her home and we went back to bed. *Now nothing else can happen today*, we said to ourselves. *We've truly had our share of emergencies for a bit.*

It was so nice to revert to our dull, dreary routine at breakfast time, but of course we all knew there would be a lot more work for John now that Roger had gone. At that time we had no idea that Richard would be leaving the excitements of lorry driving and coming back to us. As we sat at the table with the doors open, we began to hear the silage contractors arriving in the distance. The droning noise became louder and louder as an army of tractors and machinery came up the lane, and as we watched it looked like a huge disjointed green caterpillar slowly turning into our drive and crawling up towards the farmyard. We had known they would be coming some time around now, but we would have preferred to have had a quiet day today after the alarms and excursions of the previous day and night.

Silage has taken over from hay on most of the farms in Britain. Haymaking still takes place, but to a very minor degree compared to how it was years ago. The advantage of silage is that

100

harvesting can be done more quickly than for hay. You don't have all that turning for days on end to dry it—we farmers call it tedding—only for it to be rained upon, with the result that you have to start all over again. A grass crop that is going to be turned into silage doesn't need particularly dry or sunny weather before it can be cut, and it can be handled and stored very efficiently. Most of all, it has a better nutritional content than hay and is therefore particularly good for dairy cows. Sadly, it doesn't have the glorious smell of newly made hay, but we just have to accept that old methods go and new ways of farming take their place.

Some farmers buy their own silage equipment and do the whole job themselves, but these days more and more employ contractors. The latter seem to have bigger and more efficient equipment every year, and the job always seems to take less time than it did the year before. Ours used to take up to eight days to cut and gather, but with up-to-date machinery it now takes only two days to complete our usual 200-acre harvest, which is done twice each summer.

Charlie and Harold, our part-time dry-stone waller who has been with us for over twenty five years, left the breakfast table and went out for a chat with the silage men. No doubt they were catching up on recent gossip and having a bit of banter and a joke. The contractors would then take a little time to prepare the machinery, oiling the many moving parts and pouring diesel into the fuel tanks. Then they'd get going and they wouldn't be back down from the fields until about ten o'clock that night.

For me it was a normal working morning,

although I didn't need to meet the school bus as it was still the holidays. Our two had decided to go off for the day on their bikes with their friends, riding from village to village and visiting other friends on their way. So I cleared away the breakfast and went over to the office. That day I'd arranged for an older man who had recently joined the Bureau to come to the office for an interview.

When George arrived I immediately realised he was a most courteous old gentleman. He'd brought me a wonderful array of vegetables freshly cut from his garden, carefully arranged in a wicker basket, together with a lovely bunch of home-grown flowers. I thanked him and went to take the vegetables out of his basket. 'No, no, it's *all* for you,' he protested. 'Please keep it all.' He was exceedingly sprightly, with short grey hair and a lovely complexion. 'I just wondered,' he began, 'if you think it would be possible for me to meet a lady at my age. I lost my wife a year ago, and it's so very lonely. Just to be with someone and share their life and have companionship, that's all I ask for.'

George lived in the Forest of Dean, way down in Gloucestershire. By travelling to the Peak District he had demonstrated that he did not find driving difficult, so I wouldn't find myself limiting possible introductions to ladies who lived locally to him. Nevertheless I had to tell him it wouldn't be easy to find a match, because I didn't want him to have any illusions that introductions would come along as easily as they do when you are much younger.

'I know,' he said, 'but please see what you can do.'

'Well, yes. And before you go home I'll look in

102

my register just in case there's someone I could discuss with you now.'

And as I looked through my register, Nancy immediately came to mind. I told George that back in January this lady of advanced years, whom I had introduced to her previous husband way back in the 1980s, had got in touch with me again. They had, she said, been blessed with many years of happy marriage, but she was now widowed and lonely and wondered if there was any chance of meeting someone else. That request had been made over six months ago, and because of the age factor I'd not been able to introduce her to anyone yet.

'Well, I'm interested,' George told me.

Quietly I reflected that it would be an amazing thing if this one went well. They lived four hours apart by car, which—despite George's clear willingness to drive long distances—was a lot for people of their age. Their lifestyles and backgrounds could be so different. She was nearly five years older than him, and the older people get the more difficult they usually find it to be adaptable. I didn't feel at all positive, and voiced my concerns to George.

'But I really *am* interested,' he repeated.

'All right, all right, I'll talk to her about you tomorrow,' I said.

'Please do so,' he said in his typically polite manner as we ended the interview.

With my morning's work for the Bureau over, I walked from my office to the farmhouse and went mentally into my other mode, that of farmer's wife. I remembered I'd got to get supper that evening for about twelve hungry silaging men and realised I needed to go shopping for bread rolls and a few other things.

As I jumped into the car I noticed that John, surprisingly, was sitting at his desk in the farm office. I thought this was unusual, as he would normally be up the fields making sure his precious silage was 'safely gathered in'. *There must be some urgent paperwork*, I said to myself as I drove out of the yard.

When I returned two hours later John was still in the same position in the farm office. *How strange*, I thought. *I've never seen him doing paperwork before when silaging is going on, and for so long.* I went into the office and immediately realised something was wrong. He was white yet sweating. It seemed as if he couldn't speak, and yet his eyes looked at me.

'Whatever's the matter, darling?' I asked anxiously.

'I've got such a pain,' he whispered.

'Where?' I responded.

Without moving a muscle, he said he had pain in his chest and his arms were hurting.

I knew immediately what could be happening, flew to the telephone and dialled 999 for an ambulance. As I waited with John, all the aspects of resuscitation kept going through my mind. Would I really be able to do it if he collapsed? I'd resuscitated twice in my life: once it had worked, but the other time it had not.

The ambulance got there amazingly quickly considering we are so isolated and I've never been so relieved to see the emergency services arrive, even though it was for the third time in twenty-four hours. Charlie saw it from the fields, and came

104

quickly down into the farmyard to find out what was going on. It was decided he would tell the children about their dad when they arrived home, and I would telephone him when I needed a lift back from the hospital.

When we got there, John was admitted at once. Only those who have sat in a A&E department while their loved one is being stabilised in what could be a life-threatening situation know the torment that you go through. I kept saying to myself, *'I love him so much—nothing can happen to him.'* But you know that it can.

I was advised not to stay but to let John rest for the night. Charlie brought the children over to the hospital, but they weren't allowed to see their father. Charlie drove us all back home, and throughout that return journey I recalled all the years John and I had spent together since we first met on that rainy day in a sodden shed.

All couples who have been together for many years experience highs and lows in their relationships, and I thought back to ours. Lows like the accidents, and for us the struggle in our earlier years to expand and make the farm organised and profitable. I thought about the decade of struggling to have babies. I thought about the death of our first child at five years old, and how we got through that by literally clinging together. The happy times of enjoying the wonderful countryside around the farm and now having two healthy grown-up children who made our world complete. That night I prayed so hard that John would be all right.

At six the next morning I telephoned his ward to ask how he was. He was no worse, they told me, and he was stable and comfortable. What relief I felt. I went and sat for a while in a peaceful part of the farm overlooking miles of Derbyshire countryside, and said a silent thank you to whoever needed to be thanked.

John's time in hospital went well and he was released quite soon with appropriate medication. I was not, however, expecting the news that I was given when I went to pick him up. He had been lectured on his future by his consultant: 'Don't work so hard . . . change your lifestyle . . . rethink your life.' So while he was lying in his hospital bed he did just that, and started to consider some life-changing decisions. Sitting in the car in the hospital car park, he said, 'Don't drive off straightaway. I've something to tell you . . . I've been thinking about selling the herd and not milking any more.'

I thought I had heard wrong. 'What did you say?' I stuttered.

'Yes,' he said. 'If all this hard work is going to contribute to bringing my life to a sudden and early end, then the dairy cows should be sold.'

We both went totally silent for a while, and then I said I thought giving up his cows would virtually kill him anyway.

'Well, if we decide to go that way I won't let it,' he said. 'We can be sensible about it all, plan it well and keep telling ourselves it's for the best, can't we?'

'Yes, my darling, if that's what you want.'

His family had been dairy farmers throughout the twentieth century and he had never known anything else. It had always been his life: he loved his cows and was proud of the herd he had built up.

I could not imagine life at the farm without milking twice a day. Not that the twice-a-day milking routine relied on John completely. We'd been lucky compared to some farmers in that we'd always been able to employ farm workers. This meant we'd had days away, holidays even, and on the majority of days John would only milk in the morning—afternoon milking was very often done by someone else. In the winter this meant that John could finish his physical work at about five o'clock, enabling him to spend some time in the farm office or with the children. Also, since 1993 he had always taken at least one full day off a week to sit on the local magistrates' bench. He felt that being a JP was a good thing, as it got him completely immersed for some time in other aspects of life. He had to get his head around legal matters, and to involve himself in aspects of people's lives that he would not normally have to consider in farming.

But to sell the cows? I was completely convinced that it would never happen, as I just couldn't visualise him without his precious dairy herd. At home he continued to talk about it, and I just agreed with him, as you do. *Keep him happy*, I thought. *He'll change his mind*.

CHAPTER NINE

FARAWAY FOREIGN FIELDS

While the farmhouse remained the scene of constant discussions between us and the children about our future, the Bureau remained busy too. People were becoming members, having introductions and meeting people. Sometimes it worked, sometimes it didn't.

I started the Monday after John's return from hospital by opening the post and sorting through letters and new registration forms. One particular letter enthralled me immediately. It was from Iris. 'It's going incredibly well', she wrote. 'I feel we have actually fallen in love and our whole world has changed.' Iris went on to say that she had now started to stay at Mark's farm, where she got on incredibly well with his father, and that at other times Mark came to stay with her. Wow! This was a complete breakthrough, as I knew neither of them had ever become as close as this to a partner. She then went on to say Mark would be coming to stay with her this coming weekend: could they come to see me?

Oh! How lovely—it would be so nice to see them, I said to myself, and promptly telephoned Iris to arrange for them to visit us on Friday evening.

When they sat together on our settee that Friday they seemed so much in love. Mark looked at Iris as if she was the most desirable creature on this earth, and I guessed that their relationship had moved on to the intimacy and closeness that they both so much wanted. Then he told me that Iris would be on duty at the hospital on Sunday and, as he would be alone at her house, asked if he could pop up and see me for a short while.

When he arrived, he launched straight in. 'I'm worried that Iris isn't as domesticated as my mother used to be. Mother always kept the farmhouse so spick and span, and I'm sure I'll get cross with Iris if she lets the place get really untidy. But I do love her so much. What shall I do, Pat?'

I realised that this was a big issue for Mark, but I couldn't let it cause the relationship to falter. This was one of the difficulties of marrying later in life, I explained. I said he must make sure to meet Iris halfway—not to be over the top or fanatical about ultra-tidiness, and to realise that no modern-day woman would behave in the same way as his mother, who had died two years previously.

'So,' I added, 'you're thinking about making your future life with Iris, are you?'

'Yes, I want to propose to her when we're away on this holiday we're arranging to Cuba. But romantic life isn't easy, is it? I worry that there are aspects of me that she hasn't seen yet and that she won't like when she does. When I get really niggly and cross, and lose my temper because there are problems with the work on the farm, would she be able to accept that? Or would she walk out on me, even if we were married?'

'Every new thing we do in life, Mark, takes courage—and sometimes with a loving relationship you have to take that "leap of faith".' I promised I would talk to Iris about his concerns as soon as I could see her alone. In fact I think Iris suspected something, for when Mark had gone back home on the Monday she asked to come to see me.

I put the situation to her straightaway. 'Mark says that you mean more to him now than anything in the world. He loves you so much he can't imagine life without you. But he's also sensible enough to know that life's more than holding hands. He worries that his mother's ways have had a huge influence on his outlook, and he knows you're very different in attitude—for instance in the way you keep house. Would this come between you if you were together? He also worries that there are aspects of him that you won't like, and won't be able to accept too easily.' *And now*, I thought, *for some good advice*. 'Personally, I feel the problem is that you aren't communicating enough. Talk everything out, Iris. Everything can be put right with compromise. Think about a life without each other—how very lonely you would be. You don't want to go back to that, do you? So somehow you've both got to find solutions to these problems. Marriage is a very basic two-way agreement—and I do so much want it to work for the two of you.'

Iris went away in a very thoughtful frame of mind, determined to talk it all out.

Later that day I had a phone call from the Falkland Islands, way down in the South Atlantic. This might seem unusual, but in fact it isn't. The Falklands are so isolated that meeting a partner can be difficult, and I'm contacted quite often from this far-flung place. On this occasion, however, it was a little different—this time it was a lady. It was odd, because I had always thought there were more men then women on the Islands, which obviously gives women a better than average

110

chance of meeting someone.

Lucy said she didn't mind meeting a man from the UK—in fact that was what she was expecting. She went on to say that she was coming over to Britain in a few months' time and maybe she could meet up with someone then, having got to know him first by letter or phone. I accepted that this could be done. Over the years I've been successful in introducing three couples who are now married and live happily in the Falklands, where the male half came from in each case. It would be different this time, however, with the woman in the Falklands and the man in the UK.

Then about two weeks later, but before Lucy had received any introductions, I got another long-distance call, this time from East Falkland, from a man who farmed a number of miles from Port Stanley. He'd come to the UK recently with the main objective of finding a wife or companion, but had not met anyone and had returned home about three weeks ago. He felt very disheartened, but thought he might have a last chance through me.

I listened to all he had to say, then added, 'Well, before I start looking in Britain, Stephen, why don't you consider someone in Port Stanley?'

'Oh, Mrs Warren, I'd like to! But there's no one—I know everyone of around my age who's looking to meet someone.'

'Oh, yes, there is,' I insisted.

'Can't be,' he replied with equal firmness.

'Well, Stephen, I've got a lady on my register who lives in Port Stanley and is the perfect age for you—but I can't tell you anything more about her because, as you know, you will guess who she is,' I continued.

'Mrs Warren, will you talk to her about me? If you tell her my name she'll know who it is straightaway. Ask her if she would like a date.'

This is strange and a little amusing, I thought to myself. Here I am twelve thousand miles away, trying to arrange an alliance between two people who live so close to each other.

I telephoned Lucy and told her the scenario. Was there any man close by she had ever been interested in?

'No, no, no,' she said.

Then I told her about Stephen—and was met at first by complete silence.

'But I thought he didn't want another woman,' she said at last. 'He was widowed a few years ago, and whenever anyone said anything to him about finding another wife he always laughed it off.'

'Well, Lucy, he *is* interested, and if you agree I would like to organise a date for you.'

'Oh! I can't believe this—that's amazing,' she said. She then thought for a moment and added, 'There's no need for you to do that—I'll phone him and say you've spoken to me. I'm utterly astounded that he's been keeping his light under a bushel. I know him well—we've both always lived here, and I can say anything to him.'

I told Lucy that Stephen didn't know it was her I'd been talking to him about, but he *had* given me permission to tell her who *he* was (it can get quite complicated sometimes).

'Don't worry, Pat—leave it to me,' was her reply.

I was quite excited at all this because I was instigating something I'd never done before. About a week later Stephen phoned and said he couldn't believe it when Lucy had got in touch with him.

'She never indicated she wanted to meet anyone,' he said in amazement.

'There you go!' I replied. 'You never can tell about anything in life.'

Stephen went on to tell me that after her telephone call he'd gone to Stanley and they'd met up for their date. 'The trouble is,' he added, 'I know her so well it's difficult to see her in the light of romance. But she's going to travel up to the farm next week, and we'll see.'

Several weeks went by, then Lucy telephoned me with a similar reaction. 'It's not going to work,' she said. 'I just can't think about love and romance in his company. I'm sure Stephen thinks the same.'

'Never mind,' I said soothingly. 'It was worth a try. I'll now start considering a man from the UK for you and the same with Stephen—only a woman, of course!'

Because the Falklands are so windswept and desolate, and so very far from anywhere else, I've always introduced people from there to someone from a similar region in the UK. Scotland is good, of course, and Wales has proved particularly useful. Lucy was introduced to two Welsh farmers, and in the course of the next few months wrote and spoke to them both. Stephen was sent details of Jane, who had lived for a number of years on a remote Scottish island but now lived in mid-Wales. She had been a sheep farmer, like Stephen, and still had a smallholding.

It wasn't too long before Stephen got in touch. He was arranging for Jane to fly out to spend several weeks with him, and he would let me know how it all worked out. Weeks went by, then Lucy telephoned to say she was in the UK. She had met

113

both men and really couldn't decide between them, spending a little time with one, and then with the other. 'I'm having a great time,' she added. 'I won't hurt their feelings, but I just want to keep enjoying myself.' But no news from Stephen.

Other aspects of dealing with people from abroad arose when I had a request from Tony. He was in the UK at the time, but had been asked by a consortium to go out to Zambia to take control of a forestry project there for six months. He'd lived virtually all his life in Africa and had only spent a limited amount of time in Britain. Divorced about two years earlier, Tony now wondered if any lady might consider getting to know him by phone and letter while he was out in Africa. His thoughts were that, if everything went well, maybe he could come back and meet her when the six months were up.

For a lot of his time in Zambia he said he would be in the jungle sleeping rough. He suggested that I hire a global satellite system to keep in touch with him! That would be a first. One thought I had was that, if I could introduce him to a lady before he went to Africa, in the two weeks before he went out there they might actually meet. I would hate to think of them both corresponding for all those months, and getting their hopes up, to find when he returned that there was no chemistry between them. After a day considering all these implications, I decided to contact a member named Yvonne.

'Something a little unusual, Yvonne, for you to consider.' I described Tony's situation to her. I felt she was really well suited to be introduced to him. Firstly, I knew that her brother had lived in Africa for some time, so I thought she would have gained some knowledge through him. She was also a very versatile and adaptable lady, not conventional at all, so maybe Tony would appeal to her.

'Well, yes, I would be interested,' she said—in fact she seemed fascinated by the project. 'Actually,' she added, my daughter's going out to join friends in Botswana in a month's time. How close is Botswana to Zambia?'

'What a coincidence!' I exclaimed. 'Maybe the girls of your family could end up in Africa, together! Whatever you do though, Yvonne, try to meet him before he goes out there, just to see if you want to invest a lot of emotional energy into communicating with him over all those months.'

The next bit of news I had was that they had spoken twice and Yvonne had said, 'We really get on.' They then managed to meet up before he left. I've grown to like Yvonne so much, and I would be thrilled if I was part of bringing a whole new life to her—in the jungles of Africa.

And while we're on the subject of clients in distant places, what of handsome, successful Rupert with business interests in eastern Europe and his own PR? I had a call from Lynda, a girl I'd introduced him to, who complained, 'He's a complete fraud! He's told me he goes off to do business in Europe and owns racehorses. But how can he be doing all this if he's an ordinary farmer?'

I had to tell her he wasn't an ordinary farmer. He did seem to lead a very cosmopolitan life, I agreed, and he also seemed to be exceedingly wealthy. It was good that this didn't appear to impress Lynda at all—indeed, in the next telephone call she told me she wouldn't be seeing him again.

This scenario repeated itself with any lady to whom I introduced Rupert, for all that he seemed to have everything a woman could wish for in a man. All he wanted to talk about was himself, his attributes and successes, and his family. He was good-looking and intelligent, but showed no interest in any potential partner. Eventually he went off the register, astonished that 'no woman wanted him'. Which was, presumably, why he had joined the Bureau in the first place. Sadly, some people never learn.

After John's heart scare, and as the year was moving inexorably on, we decided to have a short holiday. Just the two of us, and not to anywhere exotic but just for a week in the warmth of Spain. Before I went I had a special reason for looking through the registration forms of two people who had been on my register.

David was a very warm, intuitive man. Certainly he had taken possession of his female side in the sense that he had an instinct for how others felt. He was one of those people to whom you knew you could say anything, even after only knowing him for a few minutes—you knew he would listen and be genuinely interested.

He had come to me not because he was a farmer but because he now had a life in the countryside and never wanted to go back to city living. He had originally been an actor, and for many years had played parts in various television series. He wasn't a star, but he felt fine about that; he did, however, seem to be in constant demand, and made a reasonable living. He had been born and brought up in London, and it wasn't until he was in his late forties that he found himself living a country lifestyle when he was taking part in a TV series set in rural England.

Sadly, having to be apart from his wife while they were filming deepened the gulf that had appeared between them over the years. He realised they each wanted different things in life, and after nearly thirty years of marriage and bringing up a family it was obvious that things were not going to go on as they were. It would have been different if she had had an understanding of his new lifestyle, but she didn't. They got divorced, and after buying a small village house and he really started to enjoy community life. Eventually, of course, David realised he needed to share it all with someone special.

Apparently he had never heard about my Bureau, but one evening as he was on the internet he came across my website. He hadn't been searching—it just popped on to his screen out of the blue. When he started to read it he became interested and thought, *Why not?* He decided to come to my office, because he preferred to deal face-to-face with someone such as myself. As soon as he walked in through the door we hit it off. I felt he was someone I could respect, and we didn't stop talking about everything but the subject in hand— to find him a new partner! We talked about how long I had been doing my matchmaking, and I told him that in the last year or two I reckoned I'd got so much material though my experiences with the Bureau that I could write a book. Then I added, 'But I wouldn't know how to start—I'm no good at writing. It really would be an impossible thing for me to do.'

'You must try, Pat,' he responded. 'If you don't

you'll always regret it. I want to write several books myself, and I'm sure I'll get round to it one day.'

A little time went by. David was introduced to a country lady and they went out several times, although they later decided they weren't right for each other. The one thing they had in common was the healing of animals through touch. Pauline had developed this ability over the years and David had recently found he had a gift for it. One day he telephoned me and asked, 'Have you started that book yet?'

'Well, no, not yet. I've actually sat with a blank piece of paper in front of me—but I just don't know where to begin,' I replied.

'I'll do a first page for you,' he said. 'I'll send it to you, then you must promise to continue where I stop.'

After a few days the beginning of my book came. I sat down and read it, and immediately said to myself, 'well, I wouldn't start my book like that—I would start it like this.' I then lifted the cover off my computer and started typing away. Before I knew it I had completed the first chapter of my first book—and I was amazed.

I got back to David and told him the good news. 'But I'm afraid I discarded your first page, David.'

'That's all right—I knew you would. But I banked on the possibility that you would do exactly what you did.'

We laughed, and our conversation went on to the prospect of me finding another lady for him to meet.

Elli had joined the Bureau a few weeks previously. A pretty lady in her forties, she had said she thought she was a sensitive person who also had common sense, and felt she was perceptive to others' feelings and emotions. Elli wanted to meet a countryman, although she wasn't over-keen on farmers, and I had the feeling she was extremely sceptical about her chances of success. When I spoke to her she had put a lot of emphasis on the fact that she loved classical music.

'I could only meet someone who would understand how wonderful music is to me. Can you find me someone?'

I scoured the register and found no one who had mentioned music to any extent. But when I took this out of the equation, David seemed to be first in line. I described him to Elli and asked what she thought.

'He must like classical music,' she insisted.

'All right. I'll ask him,' I said.

I can remember telephoning David and asking him about his interests in general—I didn't want to jump straight into the subject. Music didn't come up. *Oh dear*, I thought, *this isn't going to work*. So nothing ventured, nothing gained.

'Do you like classical music, David?'

'Well, yes, I do, Pat. In fact I only recently visited Vienna to attend a particular concert I'd wanted to hear for a long time.'

'That's good, David, because now you've said that I'd like to introduce you to Elli.'

I understand that from that day onwards David's life was never the same. Wonderful, warm-hearted Elli brought friendship, humour, companionship and love into his life, and could be truly described as his soulmate. They were made for each other, and since that first week they met they have scarcely been apart. She is everything he needed, and he is everything she needed, in a partner. He quickly sold his home about twenty miles away from Elli's and moved into her pretty cottage. David adopted many of Elli's interests and they both enjoyed their music together. She was a regular worshipper at the local Methodist church, and David started attending also. Elli's friends became his, and all in all their lives integrated beautifully. Quite soon I received an invitation to their wedding, followed by a small reception for about eighteen guests. I was thrilled that I had been invited to such a select gathering.

Elli looked so pretty on the day, but was obviously very nervous. She is a small lady with a mass of curly, blondish hair, and the pastel pink she wore was just right. David looked so smart in his suit, and of course the music they chose—the hauntingly beautiful music of Pachelbel—made the atmosphere of their wedding ceremony magical. The reception was a sit-down meal around one large table, which is really quite unusual. But it was also special: we all felt we were not detached from these good friends of ours, but joining in and holding their hands, as they started married life together, in a circle of love and support.

I didn't see much more of David and Elli for a while. Soon after their wedding they had decided to live in Spain throughout the winter months, and bought a villa by the coast. Then, about a year after I had first introduced them, we joined them in their new home in Spain. I really needed a break, because two days before I left for that holiday I'd finished my first book. It had taken me just over a year to write, but I was able to report to David that, on account of his badgering and relentless talk of 'Go on, have a go. Write your book, Pat', I'd actually done it.

So our holiday in Spain, in the summer of 2000, would be a time to meet up with old friends and celebrate once again our recent achievements and successes.

CHAPTER TEN

SADNESS AND CHANGE

When my first book, *Tales from the Country Matchmaker*, was actually accepted by two publishers I was elated, and quite stunned. To have a choice of publisher is beyond the wildest dreams of most first-time authors. Then to have a leading film company telephone me one Friday afternoon and ask to read my new book on Monday morning, was, I felt, quite extraordinary and unreal. The film company wanted to buy the film and TV rights before the book was even in the bookshops. Their two representatives travelled up to the farm from London and sat and drank tea on my patio one afternoon in early September.

I felt I had to be seen by them as the typical farmer's wife: rounded (which I am), rosy-cheeked (which I am), and highly domesticated, producing wonderful home-made cakes (which I do not). Amazingly, the cake I'd made looked fantastic. It had risen, was a perfect colour and smelt good. I proudly cut into it after they had both commented on my obvious baking skills, but instantly a stream of uncooked cake mixture flowed out of the middle to surround the outside of the cake like a fast-moving mini-volcano. We just sat and laughed that my cover had been blown. But they immediately raised the prospect of turning my book into a TV drama series. A leading television channel had said they were interested, and had provisionally booked an hour's slot for a Sunday night.

122

I kept laughing in absolute bewilderment that this was happening to me and to what I believed was my very ordinary existence. But it was exciting, and I enjoyed every amazing twist and turn of this strange new world. Later a scriptwriter came and spent a week with me to get a real insight into our lives. That was good fun, and I really liked her. Even prospective actors and actresses were discussed. At times others have approached me from London, suggesting even more projects, and the total unreality of it all hits me when I hear myself saying, 'Talk to my agent.'

But after all extraordinary happenings you have to get back down to earth. Once the film people had left, the following morning I went into my Bureau office to deal with all the usual comings and goings. The first person to telephone me was a client from the depths of the Cotswolds. Harry was in his fifties and I'd introduced him to Sarah, who was in her late forties. It was the first match for either of them, and he seemed really excited.

'Her dogs didn't even bark at me when I visited,' he said. 'That must mean something, as apparently they bark at everyone else! I hope their owner likes me as much as they seem to. She's a feisty, fabulous woman, you know, Pat. She rides wonderfully. You could have introduced me to hundreds of women and none would have been so good as Sarah. If this goes wrong I'll never come back to you, as there could never be anyone as good for me as her. I'll give up the opposite sex altogether—I've been euphoric since I met her, and I just can't stop talking about her. We've opened up our hearts to each other—and, my God, she *is* sexy. She's like Felicity Kendal in *The Good*

Life—petite and pretty. She'll have a go at anything. I adore her.'

I commented laughingly, 'Wow, Harry, I think you like her!'

'Well, when she phones you, Pat, will you let me know what she thinks about *me*?' Harry asked.

'Yes, I will,' I replied. 'If she lets me know her thoughts and they're not confidential I'll put your mind at rest, Harry, and let you know.'

Harry was semi-retired and living in Gloucestershire. I think he had led quite a dashing life—he'd confided to me that he had a bit of a reputation as a 'ladies' man'—but really all he wanted to do was settle down with someone special. 'Yes, I love women,' he said, 'and maybe I'm a bit of a rogue, but I've been told I'm a lovable rogue.'

I telephoned Sarah and asked about her introduction to Harry. She said, 'Well, it's going along quite nicely. He's quite different from a lot of other men—but he's nice. A sweetie really, and attractive, slim and energetic. Most of all he's a wonderful rider—he used to be a Master of Foxhounds, you know.'

I am always amused at the differing responses I get from the two sides of the same relationship. I told Harry that she seemed to like him a lot, but was being very careful in her words and was obviously not so ecstatic as he was—although she possibly felt the same as him, but described things with a little more reserve.

I thought that of all the matches I had arranged recently I could leave this one to take its own course. Experience told me that just because the enthusiasm was strong did not mean it would work.

Sometimes such highs don't need much to turn into the lowest of lows. We would just have to see.

My next caller said, 'Mrs Warren, I don't want you to find me a lady to meet—I know the lady I want to spend the rest of my life with. I've known her for eight years. It's just that I've never been able to summon up the courage to ask her out. I was wondering if I could ask you to do that for me.'

Well, that's a first, I thought. *I've never been asked to approach someone I don't know and who isn't registered with me.*

I found out that the man was just coming up to thirty and had done very well in his farming career. A tenant farmer with a large acreage in Cambridgeshire, he was set up for life with his big farm and many a man would be quite envious of him. He had a good social life, went to dinner dances and hunt balls and enjoyed all the country social life of the area—but had never found a lady to rival the girl he wanted me to contact for him. He was an outgoing man but just couldn't bring himself to ask her out in case she rejected him to his face.

I asked if she would know who he was when I spoke to her.

'Oh, yes,' he replied. 'We always talk when I see her—we talk and joke together perfectly well. It's just that I cannot, *cannot* ask her out.'

I talked to him at length about what I proposed to say and, if she said yes, where they would meet up. I wrote everything down, and at seven o'clock that evening made the phone call.

I knew it wouldn't be easy to phone a stranger and explain why I was speaking to her. She seemed nice when I introduced myself, but when I told her

125

I had been requested by an admirer to ask her out the poor girl went absolutely silent.

She then said, 'This is a joke, isn't it? One of my girlfriends has asked you to play a joke on me.'

It took a little while to convince her that this was not the case, and eventually I thought I must mention the man's name.

'He's lovely,' she said. 'I always liked him and hoped he would ask me out.'

Wow, what a relief, I thought. She went on to say they had known each other for years and whenever they met up she loved talking to him, but it usually ended up with them teasing each other and never went into 'serious' mode.

I was therefore able to arrange the date. When I got back to the man, he was incredulous to hear that she had always liked him.

'No messing about any more,' I told him. 'Now you meet up with her and get on with it.'

They did meet up, and very soon considered themselves to be in a relationship. I don't think it has led to permanency yet, but I believe all is going well.

I suppose the moral of this story is that you shouldn't assume things that you don't know, and that if you want something you should go out there and try to get it. Be a knight in shining armour and have the courage to do something that may be awkward or difficult at first, but without that you will never win the prize.

The job I like doing most of all in the Bureau office is the actual matching. Letters have to be sent out and bills have to be paid, but I really look forward to the time in the week when I put people together. First of all I make sure I have put all the new members from the last few days in the register, together with any existing member who has had an introduction that hasn't worked out and has asked to be considered for another match.

I don't use a computer in this process. I could, and years ago when I had my first computer I tried it. I felt, however, that I needed more information—intangible information that you cannot put on a computer. I need to get the feel of the person—look at their handwriting, see how they have filled everything in, and read any accompanying letters. All these are elusive factors that cannot be incorporated into any computerised system.

All the registration forms are filed in low, open filing trolleys. That enables me to take each individual trolley, sit by the side of it and handle each form easily and separately within the sections. Each age group has its own filing trolley—under forties, forty to fifty years, and then a third trolley for those over fifty. When I started the Bureau, if I had been a client I would have been filed in the first trolley, representing the youngest age group. Over the years I would have moved along the trolleys and now I would definitely be in the one for fifty-plus!

So with each person's registration form filed according to gender and age, each is then filed according to where they live, or, if it is different, the area they want to meet someone in. Scotland has three sections: North, including the Outer Islands, Central and South. I have a section for the border counties of Northumberland and Cumbria, and another for Yorkshire and Lancashire together. And, just as in the days of the Wars of the

Roses, I do occasionally get people from one of those counties emphatically saying they don't want to meet someone from the other. I then have the North Midlands, Wales, East Anglia, the South Midlands, the South West and the South East all as separate areas. The subdivisions really do reduce the people I have to consider in each case to quite manageable numbers. I always put the youngest people at the front of the subdivision and the oldest at the back. So without any difficulty, for example, I can look under South Midlands, find all the forty-one-year-old Gloucestershire ladies and easily compare them with any suitable male Bureau member in the same area. The most difficult area for introductions is the South East. I suppose it is because London and the commuter belt take up so much of that part of Britain and there are fewer country or farming-orientated people there.

When I do introductions, I like to consider all the potential partners at one sitting. I can look for an individual if necessary, but I find it far better to devote about two hours to the task and search for everyone suitable. I usually start in the South East because that, as I've said, is the most difficult area and I'm not usually going to be able to match up every lady here; but I can consider temporarily transferring them to areas outside their own if they have said they are amenable. After the South East I gradually work up the country. I tend to do the youngest age group first. With under-thirties I always have far more men, so I take each individual lady under thirty, and search for a compatible male. Any left-over girls I can transfer to the next age group of thirty to forty years, because a girl can perfectly well be introduced to an older man. But I don't transfer the younger men, as it's very rare for a man of twenty-nine to wish to meet a lady of thirty-six.

Some people might wonder at me saying that, but it's a fact that the majority of younger men seek women 'of child-bearing age'. It's awful to think that this old factor, going back to the dawn of civilisation, is still there—but it is. There are other things that affect men's preferences, too, some of them again perhaps a little old-fashioned. For instance, any woman of normal height and build, who has no children and is under thirty-five and isn't exceptionally high on her career ladder, is favoured. The absolute ideal would seem to be a lady with all these attributes who is also a nurse and has a family connection with farming. Even women who work on the family farm or directly in agriculture tend not to be as desirable, for some reason, as nurses. Men look on them as caring, homely and sensible people. Women who are in professions such as engineering or accountancy seem to be a little less favoured by men, although doctors, lady vets, solicitors and teachers are apparently more acceptable. But men tend to be wary of very academic ladies, such as lecturers and scientists.

At the end of my matching session I may have a pile of up to about fifty couples whose details I've put together. When I look at the pile I wonder how many people's lives will be irrevocably changed after I've been in touch with them. Some couples won't work out, of course—they may fall at the first hurdle if one of them refuses to meet the other. Some meet just two or three times, then

129

realise they aren't compatible. Others will continue with a friendship that may last two or three months. But then, of course, there are those others whose lives will never be the same again.

It would be wonderful to know in advance which of them, out of those whose forms I have pinned together today, will actually fall in love and live together, or marry. Which of them will have children who, had I not sat down on that particular day, wouldn't even have been conceived? It's amazing, fascinating and thrilling!

On one morning when I was doing a matching session, I had a call from a man in Lincolnshire whom I had asked to telephone a lady the day before. They were both in their late forties, and very sadly both had been through dreadfully upsetting divorces.

'I can't believe how wonderfully the conversation went,' said William. 'It didn't get off to a good start, we both didn't know what to say and stuttered quite a bit, but when we found mutual ground in talking about gundogs we were fine. She had such a beautifully soft voice—I have to say I was entranced. I couldn't believe it when I put the phone down—I felt like a teenager again. I had butterflies in my stomach, and it was like when I went out on my very first date.'

'Well, that's a good sign,' I said. 'Phone her again soon, but don't rush out and meet. Take your time and get to know each other first.'

I sat and smiled as I replaced the receiver. I had had a feeling about that couple right from the time that they had both joined about a month earlier. The one thing that had stopped me putting them together straightaway was the fact that they both had gone through such sadness with their divorces, and I wondered, with such unhappiness coming together in two people, whether they could cope— but at least they would understand each other.

Then a lady called me, and explained that she had been introduced to her husband ten years ago through me. They had some wonderful years of marriage, but then, sadly, he'd died. That was a year ago, and now she wanted to rejoin. I was quite surprised, however, when she enquired, 'I won't have to pay any more fees, will I?'

I said, 'Well, everyone has to pay the introduction fee.'

She replied by saying, 'But I paid mine eleven years ago.'

'Well, those fees you paid eleven years ago wouldn't have lasted for ever—and I did give you a good service then, in that you had a good marriage for ten years until your husband died.'

She wasn't too happy about this, so I didn't encourage her to come on to my register again. Don't get me wrong—I don't just think about the financial aspect of what I do. But I hate it when people try to take advantage and expect to receive my services, which are very thorough and well thought out, for nothing.

Another thing that influenced my decision in this case is that I have to be very careful about the number of older ladies I take on. I always get far fewer older men joining the Bureau, as do all other introduction or dating agencies—even if they don't tell you that fact. So if I weren't careful I could get a huge number of ladies in their fifties and sixties on my register, but possibly not even half that number in equivalently aged men.

My last call of that early September morning was from Anthony. He telephoned to say how very much he liked Elizabeth, whom he had first met the night before. Could I advise him what he should do from now on? She was going on holiday for a fortnight in a few days' time and he didn't want her to forget him.

Anthony was nearly forty and had never been married. Like so many men who come to me, he didn't have a terrific amount of experience with women. I told him to send her a little thank you card for the nice evening they'd spent together, and say he was looking forward to seeing her when she was back from holiday. I also suggested maybe a little bouquet of flowers would be nice. Nothing over the top—maybe just a dozen pink roses if he really wanted to make an impression.

That's a nice way to finish my morning's work, I thought, as I tidied the pile of prospective new mates and put them by the computer ready to all be written to the next day. I walked over to the house and started, as usual, to put together lunch.

John was in a mood for discussion. The same thing was on both our minds. He was not long out of hospital, and we were both concerned about his health and the future.

Since he had first mentioned that we should consider coming out of milking we had talked around the subject. It would be such a big thing to do. For thirty-eight years John had been a dairy farmer who really enjoyed his job, always taking great pride in his stock and in developing a good herd. We reared all our own calves, and the cows were never treated as commercial fodder but were valued companions. Each one had a name, unlike

132

the situation in many dairy herds now.

The problem was that, although we knew our primary consideration should be John's health, we also had a lot of newly cut silage on the farm— about 3000 tonnes in all. If we sold the dairy herd then, that autumn, we would have all this expensively produced silage going to waste. But then again, if we didn't sell up, we had to bear in mind that maybe John might get ill again because of the hard work that all dairy farmers have to undertake in winter. We had talked over the situation time and time again since he had come out of hospital, and were coming to the conclusion that we would try to take some of the work off John's shoulders by employing a bit more labour, then put the herd to auction in the spring when they had been outside for a while and got 'a shine on their backs'. That's what John seemed to want to do, and I felt compromise was the best solution. He wouldn't have to work so hard this winter, and after that his life would become a lot easier.

I deliberately didn't have any lunch that day as I'd been invited to the house of a couple called Bill and Eileen in Lincolnshire, and she had said she was going to put on the most stupendous afternoon tea for me. I suspected she had been baking all week for my visit. As you might guess I put this couple together, attended their wedding and had become very fond of them.

They now had just a smallholding, because soon after they married they decided to leave their larger farm and go into retirement, even though they were only in their early fifties. They said that life was so precious they wanted to enjoy every moment together—they felt so many years had

133

been lost when they were alone. Sad to relate, though, this couple's story illustrates the fact that not every tale has a happy ending.

I was so looking forward to seeing them, and arrived at their home at about 3 p.m. But to my utter disbelief Eileen was totally over the top in everything she said and did. She was so very different from how I remembered her, and I couldn't work it out. Then Bill took me to one side and commented that I'd obviously seen the change in her.

'Yes. Whatever's wrong?' I demanded.

'She's drunk—that's what's the matter. It's virtually every day now, and it started several months ago.'

I couldn't believe it. Bill said his life had become hell, particularly in the last two or three months. I tried to talk to her—'Something's different, Eileen, isn't it?' I enquired, in a very caring and compassionate way. But she was having none of it and utterly rebuffed my suggestion. Then, as I was talking to Bill, she ran outside, jumped into her car and just drove away.

Whatever was happening here? Last time I had seen them they were deliriously happy, quite besotted with each other—now all this. Bill seemed unable to get to grips with the situation because he still loved her so much. He really didn't know what to do for the best—he felt he couldn't chastise Eileen, and he was unable to stop her drinking. He told me she was constantly buying whisky.

Of course, what immediately concerned me was that she was driving and very much under the influence of alcohol. I explained to Bill that in all conscience I felt obliged to report her to the police. They lived not far from the M18, and if she drove on to the motorway the consequences could be unthinkable. So I telephoned 999 and explained the situation, and the police said they would try to find her and stop the car. At least my conscience would be clear—I'd done what needed to be done.

I sat for hours with Bill. The lovely cosy afternoon chatting with old friends that I had been anticipating with such pleasure had turned into a different and difficult situation. I asked him if he had realised she was a heavy drinker while they were getting to know each other, and he replied that he had known nothing about it until after they were married—yet he had known her for over a year when they did marry. He told me that, when he first discovered the secret drinking he confronted her family about it. Apparently they had known about the problem for many years, but had hoped that marriage to a good man would cure her. However, they added that they thought to a certain extent it had got worse because she was so frightened of letting him down and not being the perfect wife she so much wanted to be. She couldn't, of course, see that the drinking was achieving the exact opposite of what she wanted.

The police didn't find her, but at last her car came back up the drive. She collapsed out of it and the only thing to do was to put her to bed. Then I telephoned the police to tell them she was safely home. I departed their home that night very saddened by all that had taken place and realising how easily life for two people can change from happiness to sorrow. Some days afterwards I spoke to her, when she assured me she had visited her

135

doctor and for the first time started to have treatment for alcohol abuse.

My thoughts were totally with them both when I left their home, but quickly moved on to my appetite. I'd not eaten since breakfast, thinking I would get this promised superb country tea—and of course I'd had nothing. As I drove home I realised it was too late to have a meal in a restaurant or hotel, and there seemed to be no Little Chefs or anything quick and convenient like that around. So as I passed a fish and chip shop I couldn't resist stopping and going in. Surprisingly, it had a sit-down part, and although I wouldn't normally sit in what was quite a grotty fish bar, tonight I thought, *Why not?* We'd just got a new car, and I certainly didn't want the smell and possible mess of fish and chips inside it. I was so hungry that I really enjoyed a rather greasy and totally unhealthy fish supper by myself that Saturday night, accompanied by several drunks just coming out of the pub. I had to laugh at my situation. Whatever do you get yourself into, Pat?

I was so weary when I got home, and very sad when I thought of the couple I'd been with that day. I saw two people trapped together through their love for each other. I felt particularly sorry for Bill: he was very unhappy with the situation, and it had certainly taken all the life and sparkle out of him. Most times when I feel a little despondent, which thankfully isn't often, I like to sit down with a nice glass of red wine or a gin and tonic and that usually does the trick. But I didn't dare do that when I got home that night. Would I turn into an alcoholic if I sat alone and drank? Maybe drinking alone was the prelude to what poor Eileen was going through.

Thankfully, my natural optimism returned in the next few days, but my mood at breakfast the next morning was still tinged with melancholy. It wasn't helped when John announced that he was going to ask the local auctioneers to visit the farm to discuss the sale of the dairy herd next spring.

'Best to get the date settled now,' he said.

Sadly, I agreed.

That same week the auctioneer called, and he and John both thought the end of May would be a good time.

'Well, what day in May do you think, John?' the man asked. John thought for short while, then replied that it really didn't matter—it was actually his birthday on the 22nd.

'That would be a good omen, then, John,' he said. 'The 22nd it will be.'

Once his car had disappeared down the drive we looked at each other and realised nothing would ever be the same again, and with this John suddenly became quite down in spirit. Maybe it's a common reaction when a life-transforming decision is made. He had reached this one knowing that it was the most sensible thing to do health-wise—but that kind of reasoning doesn't stop the emotional side taking over. He looked inward, and seemed not to want to take part in family life. Nothing I did or said was met with any enthusiasm, and it was altogether a very negative and depressing time.

Then one day, that autumn, without thinking much about what I was saying, I suggested 'It's our twenty-first wedding anniversary at the end of the month—how about a party?' The thought of a party seemed good to me—maybe it would drive away his low spirits.

To my complete amazement he said, 'Yes, that would be a good idea. After all, it's something to celebrate nowadays.'

I really hadn't expected him to react in such a positive way and couldn't help but show my feelings. 'That's wonderful,' I said excitedly, 'I'll get on and organise it immediately!'

So on Michaelmas Day 2000, twenty-one years after we were married, we had our anniversary party. Our friends arrived at the farm for drinks and then a four-course meal was served at a sit-down wedding-type reception. The drink flowed and the food was great. John then made a fabulously humorous speech and we cut a two-tier wedding cake. We spent the rest of the evening drinking and socialising outside on the lawn and having a really good time. This lovely occasion really set us up, and John became his usual good-humoured self again.

CHAPTER ELEVEN

MARY AND JOSEPH

It seemed no time at all after Michaelmas Day that December was upon us. I'm always very busy with the Bureau at that time: at Christmas so many people are desperately eager to meet someone special. They remember seeing other couples having a good time together, and can't bear the thought of being left out for yet another year. The festive season seems to emphasise the family bliss that we are all supposed to enjoy, and when you aren't in that situation and want it so much, your whole life seems empty. I know of one Welshman who always leaves his farm for his married brother to look after and goes away on holiday at Christmas—just so that he doesn't have to face the continual sorrow of being alone.

It's lovely to start receiving Christmas cards in early December. The senders usually say a little about how their relationship is progressing. Others enclose photos of their latest children. Of course, I also get them from couples I have unfortunately long forgotten, and I sit there—as I suspect we all do—looking at the names on the cards, quite unable to remember who they are.

About two weeks before Christmas I stop sending letters out and constantly telephone people—it concludes introductions more quickly. I would never want anyone to be waiting over the holiday period just for a telephone number without which they couldn't get in touch with the match they had previously agreed.

A very old friend of mine, Barbara, phoned up a week before Christmas in absolute desperation. She was organising the nativity play which is performed in the church in one of our larger nearby villages every Christmas Eve. She had had her teenage Mary and Joseph in place for weeks, but that day the arrangement had fallen through as they'd been invited out of the area for Christmas and wouldn't be able to take part.

'Would either of your children play Mary or Joseph?' she implored.

'I wouldn't think so,' were my first words. 'You know, they aren't children who ever wanted to be in school plays—but I'll mention it to them.'

That day, when my daughter and her boyfriend Dan were sitting round the kitchen table, I brought up the subject.

Immediately Dan said, 'I wouldn't mind doing that. I was never chosen at school to be Joseph, and I always wanted to be.'

I couldn't believe what I was hearing—great. Now to convince Sarah.

'I suppose so—if he's doing it, I'll have to.'

Well, that didn't seem to have been too difficult. It was all set—they would be Joseph and Mary. I telephoned Barbara back and she was overjoyed that this big problem had been solved.

The next few days went quickly and costumes were tried on. They had a dress rehearsal and everything seemed all right. Sarah was extra-moody one day, but I put it down to 'teenagers'. When she came home from school she was all excited, then started to tell me that she and her boyfriend had fallen out the previous day.

'But you can't do that,' I protested. 'You're Mary and Joseph very soon—you *can't* fall out!'

'Well, it's all right, Mum,' she replied, 'because we've made it up. Rather well, actually. Do you know what he did? He came to the school bus bay, and just before I got on to the bus he went down on one knee, in front of everyone, and asked me to make it up with him. Virtually all the kids at the school watched, and everyone applauded when I said yes—even the bus drivers. Then he gave me this big bunch of roses.' She produced it from behind her back to show me.

'Wow! I wish a young man would go down on one knee for me,' I said to her.

But on Christmas Eve morning Sarah came banging into the kitchen and announced with the drama that any teenager can muster, 'We've fallen out completely now. That's it, that's the end, we're not going to see each other again.'

I thought for a moment she was talking about a girlfriend—maybe unconsciously I was desperately wishing this to be the case. But no, she wasn't talking about a girlfriend. 'Which friend is it?' I asked.

'It's him,' she yelled.

'But you can't fall out with him *again*. He's your Joseph for this afternoon.'

'Well, I can and I have,' she shouted back. Do teenagers ever think of the consequences of any of their actions?

'But you'll have to make it up—you can't let people down for the play.'

At that moment her father walked in, having heard the tail end of the argument from outside. To Sarah there was no predicament—just a black

141

and white situation. They had fallen out, they weren't going to see each other again ever, and that was it.

'You've got to make it up,' John and I exclaimed in unison. 'You've just got to.'

You would have thought that a complete breakdown in world order had happened in our house. We couldn't go on to the next task of the day—and so much has to be done on any Christmas Eve. I made no food for the next day, I delivered no presents and I did no housework. Mary and Joseph just had to make their quarrel up—how could I face everyone in the villages round about, knowing that my daughter had deprived them of their annual play?

I telephoned her boyfriend. I talked to Sarah— her dad talked to her, her brother talked to her. Then at last, at 3 p.m., a breakthrough was made. Over the phone they made up and the light came into our life again—world order was restored and Mary and Joseph became friends once more.

The nativity play went off splendidly except that little baby Jesus, played by the eight-week-old newest parishioner in our village, cried all the way through and Joseph and Mary were at their wit's end to shut her up. They rocked baby Jesus, they talked to baby Jesus—but serenity was not easily acquired because the real-life donkey, who was brought into the church every year from his field about half a mile away bit the sheep (yes, real sheep from the field at the back of the church were always used) and there was blood everywhere in the manger scene where Joseph and Mary sat with this screaming baby.

I knew, from Mary and Joseph's comments

afterwards, that the experience had put them off having children for life. But I wasn't sure if it was the screaming infant, the fighting animals, their previous fall-out or a combination of these things that eventually led to them breaking up for good.

Christmas Day on the farm is really not very different from a normal weekend day. The milking and feeding still have to be done, but we always try to make sure everything is finished as early as possible on Christmas morning. We realised that year that all future Christmases would be different without a dairy herd, but that was beginning to be looked upon with a positive attitude and we appreciated the fact that less work and stress would definitely be better for John.

On Boxing Day I had a phone call from Patrick, who first asked if I remembered him. I did, because I pride myself on knowing something, no matter how small, about every current Bureau member. I'd spoken to him about three times over the last five months. He was calling from Australia, where he was on holiday. I was bewildered: why would anyone want to think about me while they were enjoying a lovely holiday in the sun in such a glorious country?

In his mid-fifties, Patrick was of Irish decent, six foot tall and broad with it, and had come over to the UK in the seventies. To start with he was a typical Irish worker in the building trade, taking on jobs all over the country and especially on the motorways. But soon Patrick began to make plans, and got it into his head that if he bought an earth-moving vehicle of his own he could earn more money than being employed to drive one. This was the beginning of what had become a very successful earth-moving and commercial plant hire business that operated nationwide and employed scores of people.

Patrick had married very young in Ireland and when he came to Britain left his wife back home with the understanding that, when he had got established, she would come over with the children. But this never happened, because she couldn't bring herself to leave Ireland and her extended family. By the time he was heading for his forties they had virtually become strangers and he knew the only solution was a divorce. Patrick wanted to meet someone else, but his business commitments and determination to succeed always got in the way.

Deciding that he needed to relax a little, he bought a lovely farm in the South East just to enjoy the peace and quiet of his own land all around him. He started to have holidays, sometimes going abroad and at other times seeing some of the remoter parts of the British countryside where his earth-moving plant was required. By his fifties he'd made himself take up a few hobbies. He became passionate about music and enjoyed learning to play different instruments. But he still hadn't met anyone who was special in his life, and this was his greatest source of disappointment. He was planning to retire soon and hoped to see the world—but, hopefully, with a partner beside him.

Patrick had come to see me in September 2000. I had looked through my register and suggested he met Charlotte, a schoolteacher from Kent who was a little younger than him. However he was quite convinced it made no sense for him to meet anyone as educated as a teacher.

'But you have a lot to offer her, Patrick,' I told him: 'Please consider it. You're a sincere, good man who has made a great success of your life. You've developed hobbies and interests, and you want to travel and have a good retirement.'

After a long while he said he'd reconsidered and would go ahead—but added that he was very sceptical that such a well-educated lady would like him, although it was nice that, like him, she had an interest in music. So their first introductions went ahead in October. I crossed my fingers and toes, but didn't hear any more from either of them until I got a Christmas card from Patrick saying he would be in Australia for Christmas but nothing more. I phoned him. I wanted to ask how the friendship was, and hoped I would catch him before he went to Australia. But I got no reply and so presumed he'd already gone. Anyway, here now on Boxing Day was Patrick on the phone from Australia. He said, 'I'd always wanted to come here for Christmas, and this year I've done it.'

'I'm very pleased for you, Patrick,' I said. 'What made you actually decide to take the holiday?'

'Oh, Pat, it's all through Charlotte. She's so wonderful and she originates from Australia and most of her family are here. So by December I'd decided—if she wanted to—that it would be good to have a holiday together here. We've stayed with most of her family and had a great time. We spent Christmas Day with her brother on his farm . . . I just thought you'd like to know what's happened to us.'

Then Charlotte came on the phone. 'He's a wonderful man. We'd both like to thank you so much, Pat, for introducing us to each other. I don't think anything will part us now.'

That's so nice, and they will both be able to look back at a lovely Christmas, I said to myself when the conversation finished and I put the phone down.

Most years, as soon as the festive season is over I plan the forthcoming couple of days I spend in London to attend the Annual General Meeting of the Association of British Introduction Agencies. I feel it's important to belong to your trade association to get feedback from other agencies and generally make sure you are up-to-date on legislation and the various professional guidelines that you should adhere to.

The AGM lasted most of the day—quite a boring event, as most AGMs are, but it was nice to see the people I had got to know over the years. Just as I was leaving, John phoned me to say someone from *The Times* would be getting in touch with me at 6 p.m. to do an interview on my mobile for a long feature about the Bureau that they wanted to run in the next few days. This would be extremely good publicity and you only get that sort of chance occasionally, so I was very keen to make the most of it. The problem was that it was nearly 6 p.m. now and I was walking down Regent Street where the traffic was very loud—I needed somewhere quiet to sit down and speak (and indeed listen) to whoever would be phoning me. I walked into several cafés, but they'd all got loud music playing in the background. I was desperate. On the dot of six I just sat down on a seat outside a café and took the call. It was tremendously noisy, but somehow I managed to do this important interview reasonably well despite everything.

They wanted a colour photograph of me to

accompany the article, so once I was back home they sent a make-up artist from London to spend the day at the farm. Make-up artist—wow, I've *really* arrived! She spent about two hours on me— *This is the best I'll ever look,* I thought. But the photo shoot was torture.

Then I waited anxiously for the article to come out. You never know in such circumstances what they will say about you: it could be complimentary, or it could be highly critical. The journalist quoted what I said I'd told one man who confessed he hadn't 'entertained a lady' for many years and was worried about his performance. 'It's like riding a bike,' I told him, and assured him he'd soon remember how everything fitted into place once he got going. *That was a bit explicit,* I thought in retrospect. They also quoted me as saying, 'You've got to take a deep breath and it's the same if you're eighteen or forty-eight. You've got to have a go at life.'

With their permission, *The Times* had interviewed one of my successful couples. The story went: 'Felicity and Philip are a perfect match. She is a music teacher and a hobby farmer, and he is a farmer and has music as a hobby.' They only lived about seven miles apart, and had told the interviewer that they had actually gone to the same primary school. The piece went on to say that Felicity, forty-seven, who lived with her elderly parents, had joined the agency wanting to meet a bachelor. Philip, fifty, had lived for years with his widowed mother, and after her death he couldn't bear the silence. The couple now lived on Philip's 200-acre farm but constantly visited Felicity's smallholding, where she kept two cows, four horses and some sheep. At the time of the interview they were celebrating three months of marriage.

Felicity was quoted as saying, 'When we first met in a restaurant it was amazing—we had so much in common. He was such an exceptionally nice person, so gentlemanly, sensible and practical. He really is quite special.' Philip said he wished they had met ten years ago so that they could have had more time together.

At the end of the article was a quote from me that I'd had to make up on the spot in Regent Street at rush hour. They asked me to articulate some wise thoughts to give to any couple. Printed in a separate box in bold type and headed 'Warren's Way', they went as follows:

'After falling in love, write down what you adore about your partner. When the going gets tough, read it and remind yourself what made you fall in love with them.
'Remember no one is perfect.
'Never go on looks, think about the person.
'When things go wrong, don't be rash. Think about living life alone.
'Spend Sunday afternoons in bed together and make love.'

Even given all the time in the world and a place of utter tranquillity in which to marshal my thoughts, I don't think I could have improved on this advice.

CHAPTER TWELVE

PAROCHIAL AFFAIRS

There is probably nothing like testing out your relationship by spending Christmas with the family of your loved one. If you still love them after that, as Patrick certainly did, usually all is well for the future. But quite a number of relationships that seemed good in the autumn had floundered over Christmas that year and I received several messages along these lines: 'Put me back on the register. I'm afraid I couldn't stand his/her friends and certainly not his/her family.' 'I never want to spend another Christmas alone. I'm applying to you now so you have twelve months to help me rectify the situation,' came another cry.

So, typically, I buckle down after most Christmases and AGMs and have a lot of days of hard work. But most Januarys I also do a bizarre thing and sit in a draughty village hall for what seems like an interminable length of time. The hall is usually cold, as the ceilings are high and the heating ancient. People take rugs to wrap round their feet, put gloves on when entering the place and wear three pairs of socks. Cushions are advisable: the chairs are mostly small and hard, being left over from years ago when the building was the local school. But the reason for my being there is a part of rural life that I wouldn't miss for the world.

I know many people wouldn't want any connection with something as unexciting, insular and petty as a parish council. They say, 'Leave them alone to get on with it—little Hitlers, just wanting to hear the sound of their own voices! I'll have nothing to do with them.' But a few years after I had settled into my community I happened to go to a parish council meeting. My children were very little and tucked up in bed, and John was babysitting. Amazingly, I found it interesting—and very amusing and entertaining. Yes, parochial it certainly is, but it's at the base of our democracy. People must think me a very sad character—can I really not find anything more stimulating to fill my evening once a month than attending a meeting in a freezing village hall? But it's so full of what life is made up of: people with different views, attitudes, lifestyles and prejudices, all set against a backdrop of the land where we live and its history.

So when the children were little, as a break from the house I started to sit in the audience at parish council meetings. Yes, I could have gone to evening classes to learn to speak Russian or to play the trombone. But it was easy just to travel the short distance to the village to meet people I had not seen for a while and with whom I shared local interests. At every meeting a vast audience would be hoped for, and row upon row of chairs would be religiously set out. But no, you don't have a hope in hell of filling even one-tenth of them. You'd be lucky, even if the whole of the television broadcasting system had broken down and the sun was shining on every yard of roadway leading to the village hall and a man was standing at the door giving out fivers, to get more than seven.

In those early years, I was full of admiration for the chairman and clerk. They seemed to exude proficiency and capability: I was truly in awe of these 'elder statesmen'. My part in the proceedings consisted merely of chatting with other farmers' wives for possibly the first time in several months, getting to know about some of the local issues and coming back to tell John all about it at the end of the evening.

Of course, the inevitable happened; wiser and less naive folk than me would have anticipated it. One day the parish clerk decided to resign. He was a man with whom I'd always got on well and, although he was regarded as an absolute eccentric in the village, I liked him a lot. And yes, he suggested that his successor should be me. I was completely taken aback and quite unconvinced that I could perform what I regarded as an esteemed and prestigious job. Yes, in those days I was young and impressionable.

Nevertheless I flung myself head-first into the work—and quickly realised how utterly disorganised the previous incumbent had been. So, sadly, my regard for this gentleman was somewhat dented and I settled down to what I now realised were the lacklustre duties of the parish clerk. At once I saw my fellow-members in a completely different way—but after all, I was now on the top table.

Our village is a very pretty one with a long history. In Victorian times, a famous archaeologist lived here: he built the hall and all the estate cottages that stand around the square. He did lots of excavations around the area, particularly at Arbor Low, and most of his findings are to be seen in Sheffield Museum. He was proud of his achievements, and as his life drew to a close he was

151

anxious to choose an appropriate resting place for his body. He had built a Methodist chapel in the village, and decided that his grave must lie near by. In due course he was buried in a corner of the field adjoining the chapel, resting quietly beneath a substantial stone tomb surrounded by iron railings and guarded by dark yew trees. The final resting place of Squire Bateman became the subject of a parish council meeting when a tourist complained that she couldn't get to his grave because the path was so overgrown with nettles.

When we came to discuss the matter, the debate went back and forth as usual—whose responsibility was it, how often should it be cleared, who would actually do the work and who would pay? And, of course, we meandered down memory lane. Someone recalled how small the yew trees had been when she was a girl, and then someone went even further back and said his grandfather had been Squire Bateman's coachman, and then the debate started to turn to his diggings and what the squire had found. There were at least three people at the meeting who seemed to possess some Stone Age treasure that their great-grandparent or great-uncle had turned up when they were ploughing. Eventually we got to the point again, and it was agreed that a committee would be set up to get the grave site cleared and repaired. Business was closed, and we got up stiffly from the little chairs. I closed my clerk's notebook, wrapped myself up in my winter coat and scarf, and headed home.

When I got back to the farm, John was busy roasting his toes in front of the roaring log fire. He asked what had happened at the meeting. I told him that if he was that interested he should have gone himself, I was too tired to go through it all again and he could read the minutes! In fact my intention was to type them there and then, because I was going away the next day and wanted to distribute them before I went. I hurried through them, ran the spell check over the text and printed them off. Too tired to bother to read them through, I turned off the computer, climbed the stairs and sank gratefully into bed—and oh, heaven, John was lovely and warm to cuddle up to.

On my way through the village next day, I hurriedly pinned the minutes on the notice board for all to read. I also dropped a copy off with the editor of the parish magazine in the next village. His knowledge of Squire Bateman is limited as he's a newcomer to the area, but I know he's always very keen to get material. He used to be in advertising, I think, so he tends to go for the eye-catching headline.

I had a good trip, visiting some friends over the next few days, and the parish meeting was completely forgotten about. On my return I walked into the kitchen and John asked me whether I'd seen any unusual people in the village on the way through. Then he handed me the newly printed parish magazine and rolled around with mirth. The front page bore the headline 'BATMAN'S GRAVE DISCOVERED'. Who would be without the benefits of a spell check facility when it can give you treasures like this!

I do, in fact, rely heavily on the spell check, for my inability to spell is legendary. When I was writing my first book, my good friend Jill was reading through the chapter about the party for the Bureau's twenty-first anniversary. She looked up from the kitchen table and exclaimed, 'Gosh, Pat, you must have had big tables at the party—vases of sweet-smelling Freesians would take up a lot of space!'

The most embarrassing mistake I ever made as parish clerk was when I put some information on disks and sent them out, in advance of the meeting, to those who I knew had computers. After the meeting someone took me aside and said he wondered if I was in the right business, as maybe my knowledge of sex was limited. I looked at him in astonishment—whatever was he on about? Then he pointed to a paragraph in the instructions I'd given out: 'When you have read the instructions then insert your floppy diks.'

At parish council meetings our chairman is always first to arrive. The importance of his position is of course paramount, and he sets out the table and chairs as he wishes—so one could say his influence is immediate! He then takes a seat. All the council members seem to have their preferences, and there is much manoeuvring to obtain their desired position around the table and their favourite chair. Most prefer the soft ones, which are few in number and prized considerably. All the rest are small, extra-hard and upright—so God help you!

The chairman gets his hearing aid box out of his pocket and sets it on the table in front of us all like an exhibit in court. Alongside go his glasses, and I'm always expecting his teeth to be produced too. The hearing aid is inserted and the usual ringing noises begin, so he takes it out and taps it on the table and then puts it back in his ear, adjusting the position. Right, at last he's ready. Then, just as we all feel he's got everything set up and ready to go someone says something to him and obviously the volume is set far too high. He jumps out of his chair with the shock, and the whole process of adjustment and ringing noises starts all over again.

Pens and pencils are extracted from pockets by all, minutes of the previous meeting are dropped by at least half, then we have the usual screeching of chairs being pushed back and bums elevated while their owners squat under the table to retrieve them. The noise factor—from possibly no more than twelve people—reaches a crescendo as chairs are once again put in place and the previously mentioned bums are positioned on the said chairs while they are all screeched from side to side.

The meeting is opened and we begin. Always, always, someone comes in late. They apologise and take their seat and we begin the meeting all over again.

Since I first started participating I've been elevated first to councillor and then to the lofty position of vice-chairman, but I really do still only attend for the entertainment value. I'm afraid I cannot take anything too seriously, even though some will think badly of me for this. I admire it absolutely as part of our historic democratic process, but always try to keep a sense of balance: nothing we decide upon is that important, really.

To get back to the meeting: once again there is a delay in proceedings by a round-the-table offer of a Polo mint. Virtually everyone has one, and the chobbling and the crunching seem to vibrate around the room to the chairman's confusion, then annoyance.

'Let's get to business,' he says testily. He asks a

question, and nobody answers. He repeats the question: 'What shall we do about the big key?' The subject in hand is produced: the big key is put in the middle of the top table just like any exhibit in a court of law. It is a very big, old key. Someone picks it up and it is passed around and looked at as if it has fallen from Mars. Then a voice says that we should get it copied. 'Who will do that?' enquires another voice. A name is suggested and 'yes, he would be a good man' is the reply we get from most, repeating what each other has said as if we were a bunch of cloned monkeys. It is the key to our very old parish safe, and we want to get a duplicate!

Then comes the next big decision: 'Who is going to keep this key safe?' No one answers. No one wants this almighty responsibility. We all shuffle our feet and lower our eyes. Then it's decided by the chairman, as he obviously doesn't want this burden and tells the clerk that it has to be her.

That subject over, we get another bout of coughing when the Polos are passed round again and more sucking starts. Just as we are about to get to the next topic, in comes another late arrival. She is a new inhabitant of one of the more remote farmhouses and, good on her, at least she puts herself out to attend and has a great interest in the community. Lucy has a lot of children and I secretly suspect she comes along as an excuse to leave most of the kids with Dad and have a break. I say 'most' because she always brings the youngest with her.

Lucy has had three children in the last three years, so like all busy mums she knows the value and convenience of breast feeding. Now it solely

156

depends on whether the child in her arms is asleep or not, but if not you know the first thing she will do—really to keep the offspring quiet as much as for any other reason. You can read the collective minds as they are guessing if it will be the left or right side first. Sometimes baby will feed with great noisy gulps that seem to embarrass every man present. They all seem completely mesmerised by the whole process and utterly distracted by the high-pitched sucking sounds from the issues under discussion. I think Lucy is great, and long may every harassed and busy mother sit down, rest and relax, chat with neighbours and friends and feed her babies—at every parish council meeting in the country.

Next on the agenda: holes in the wall along the main road in the village. It is always the same good lady who brings this subject up, as she has made it her mission in life to see that we have well-kept walls. Of course we all get fed up with it and certainly the clerk does, but good old Elaine keeps this issue going. So many would have given up the fight with the Highways Dept, but our true crusader does not.

'We've been trying to do that for ten years,' someone says, 'but let's try again.' And so 'Another letter please, clerk'—*Thank God I'm not still the clerk*, I say under my breath. I'd had enough of that onerous duty after six years, so about three years ago I resigned. The problem is you don't realise how noisy you still are about the meetings once you've given up. So I'm now a parish councillor.

Anyway, I needn't have said *Thank God I'm not still the clerk* under my breath, as the majority in the room wouldn't have heard—there are constant

157

rumblings of 'You what? . . . What did they say?' from the small audience as most of them are somewhat deaf, a situation not helped by the fact that they are trying to listen to the proceedings over the crunching of Polo mints and the slurping of infant refreshment. So we have several conversations going on at the same time, providing a complex web of discussion that confuses the hard of hearing even more.

'. . . financial position'—the usual councillor proclaims his continued interest in this subject. A good political man, absolutely for the people and preserving public money at all costs! We should all be proud of him as he makes sure not a penny is spent needlessly. He restrains any squandering or overspending and really ought to have a position in the Cabinet or Treasury. The country would be able to save millions, and instead of paying tax the whole population could be given a holiday, totally paid for by the efforts of our very own Mr Careful.

Parish bills have to be paid, even so—but the appropriate chequebook is not to hand. The lady who keeps the chequebook says she will fetch it, so we all wait in anticipation while she pops home. The Polos are passed round again, and baby is changed to the other side.

She comes back into the village hall only to find she's brought the wrong chequebook. One or two are putting their gloves on and wrapping their rugs more tightly around them. Eventually, as we start to discuss our money situation, the chairman's hearing aid gives up the ghost. From now on he has to cup his hand around his ear to make the necessary 'trumpet' and 'You what?' is uttered a hundred times throughout the rest of the meeting.

It's amazing, though, that he can hear when another councillor says to me across the table, 'I'll bring those jam jars and vinegar over to you tomorrow', and reprimands us for talking about non-parish business. A bit of gossip comes up and everyone earnestly pricks up his or her ears. 'It's only sex,' someone says—obviously describing the latest liaison of a well-known male from another village and a female from ours. 'She was up a ladder to his bedroom—not sure if she was getting out or trying to get in.'

The chairman asks what we have all just said. 'It's only sex' is repeated to him by about four councillors at the same time, so he's totally confused about what has been decided at this parish council meeting and asks if that is being minuted.

Then a disagreement occurs because someone had said, 'Those kids don't deserve any more play equipment. I never had any when I was young.' It is then suggested that a formal letter be sent to the clerk of the village hall committee about not spending any more money on the children.

'Well, that's me,' says our very own parish clerk. 'You know I'm village hall secretary as well.'

'Well, never mind,' says a councillor. 'We want a formal letter sent.'

The clerk nods her head, but with an expression of disbelief. 'So I've got to write a letter to myself formally complaining, and it will be up to me to answer it myself!'

All agreed. Yes.

I love it—it's great, and you honestly could never make any of this up. Just as we think nothing else can happen, there's a knock on the door. It's pitch black outside and we all wonder who it could be. In comes a lady whom none of us know; she introduces herself as someone staying overnight in the camping barn.

'I'm in a predicament,' she says. 'I've only got this tin of pears to eat, and I've no tin opener. Could you open the tin for me?'

We are all quite astounded. Never has a request like this been made before at our meetings, but we dutifully help the lady and on her way she goes. We were quite sad that all she had to eat on a freezing cold night was cold tinned pears.

To wind up the meeting we hear a colourful account of a fight that broke out among three bulls when they got out of their respective fields and had an almighty battle in the middle of the road in the village. We are spellbound by the story, including the equally colourful details of the way the neighbouring farmers defended their precious animals.

The meeting ends at ten o'clock and we all go home to people who, had they been watching the latest comedies on TV, would not have been so richly entertained, amused or informed as we have been at our two-hour parish council meeting.

That cold January night in 2001, as I drove the short distance home, I thought how hilarious some aspects of our recent parish business had been. Hilarious because it can be taken so seriously, so earth-shatteringly and on a par with world events, by so many—though, as I have mentioned, not by me. The referendum was one such situation.

Referendum—you might think they are only held in connection with weighty matters such as the EU. No, no, no, I can assure you they are not so restricted. Our village had a referendum a few years ago. So perhaps it was over a very important issue, an issue that was paramount to the whole life and progress of the community? Well, no—it was about whether the village should have a public toilet or not. The parish council decided in their wisdom that a referendum was necessary for this big decision and, being the parish clerk at the time, under the direction of the parish councillors I was the one who had to organise the distribution of the referendum papers to all registered electors and the eventual collection and counting of the voting slips.

The village was totally divided on the matter, which was the sole topic of conversation throughout the preceding weeks. Shall we? Shan't we? What do you think? Are you in favour or not? The parish council had decided that they were in favour and had put forward to the local authority plans to convert a disused stone shed adjacent to the children's playground. But since so many local people had such strong feelings on the subject, the council decided that an open planning meeting should take place.

The village hall was opened for the night and I arrived quite early because I had to take the minutes and wanted to be ready. The chairman of the parish council got there at the same time, and we both remarked on the possibility that no one would turn up—maybe none of the villagers would leave their TV for that evening. We all know that people can be 100 per cent in earnest about a certain issue, but when it comes to airing their views in public they often can't be bothered.

I stood at the window and looked down on to

the main street. No one was to be seen. Then, as the chairman came and stood by my side, I looked again in total disbelief. A crowd of people stretching from one side of the road to the other, and several rows deep, was moving up towards the hall like a lynch mob in a Western. I could feel his disbelief and tension when I looked at the chairman's face. Was this going to be middle England, full of politeness and civility, or would lawlessness prevail this evening?

As the crowd continued to approach, the rest of the parish council, who had by now arrived, witnessed the scene and were quite unnerved. When the first line of people opened the hall door we put on smiles as they all tumbled in, hoping they would not string us up immediately. The chairs were quickly occupied, and when the chairman decided to coax the audience into attention you could have heard a pin drop.

Since it was an open meeting everyone was allowed to express his or her viewpoint: such passion and anger, such issues and diverse thoughts. The quiet people of the village spoke— even those who had hardly murmured a word in public for years. Some thought it was a marvellous idea. It would stop visitors to the village knocking on doors and asking to use their toilets. (I was amazed that people actually did this—I know I'd rather die than ask a complete stranger if I could use their loo.) It would also stop visitors using the very pretty dale for their excreta and leaving toilet paper around for dogs and children to pick up. *God! We* are *getting basic now. I've never seen this— but then maybe on my walks around I go with my eyes closed*, I thought.

The opposite argument was that more visitors would come into the village. They'd use the toilets, block up the centre of the village with their cars, and be there lurking in the public loos to pervert the little children of the village in the adjoining playground.

Fists were banged. One or two people walked out. Passions were erupting. The parish council were amazed at what had hit them, but we had a suggestion: a referendum! It was decided that a suitable question would be written out and each adult would be given a ballot paper on which they would indicate whether or not they thought we should have a public toilet.

In the course of the next few days the forms were typed out and distributed. I thought about the preparations I would need to make. Where would the completed papers be put? Oh! Of course, that old black tin box, that's as close as you could get to a ballot box. It was stationed in our hallway, and as each slip was given or brought to me it was dutifully put into the black box. Now I had to think about the day they would be counted. I decided to co-opt the 'top brass' of the village, or rather those who definitely could count without using their fingers.

The vicar was approached, and the chairman of the parish council of course, then our *real* 'top brass', our very own Major General, born and bred in the village, who had returned in retirement. I felt he must be able to count well, for throughout his career no doubt he would have had thousands of troops under his command. I was there hosting the occasion and John (our very own magistrate) was there. A prestigious turn-out, don't you think, to count and verify the maximum 120 slips of paper that could have been returned?

They all arrived on the appointed day at four in the afternoon. After a cup of tea, a piece of cake and a chat the big black box was ceremoniously opened and the referendum papers counted and double-checked on our dining room table. It was close, we were advised. With bated breath we awaited the results, and eventually the vicar took charge and announced to the gathering, 'Exactly 100 papers have been returned. Twenty people obviously felt they did not wish to air their views; 49 are for having the toilets, and 51 against.' Then, 'Quickly type up the results,' he called out to me. 'There will be no public toilets in our village.'

Everyone relaxed as I prepared the document to be placed on the village notice board.

'Wow, the tension is too much,' said John. 'Let's get away from here.' Quickly we got in the car and had a meal out that night.

When we returned to the farm, pushed under our door were three ballot papers. I could see who they were from and immediately telephoned them. 'I'm sorry, but the referendum has been counted and the decision is on the notice board.

'How come?' came the reply. 'Ballot papers should be accepted up until midnight on voting day—you never said on your notices that there was an earlier deadline.'

I started to protest.

'No, no, you have to count them,' was the instant reply.

With that I asked the others, who reluctantly confirmed that I had to bow to the power of the ballot box and change the referendum results to

164

read 52 for having toilets and 51 against. The ayes have it.

To this day I would not dare to reveal how I voted—some neighbours might never talk to me again if they thought I was in a different camp from them on such a weighty matter. The subject is ingrained in the history of our village and still has a strong following on both sides. If you wish to get the blood flowing in our little village square, just mention the referendum.

CHAPTER THIRTEEN

LOVE IS A MANY-SPLENDOURED THING

Country women often achieve far more than men. If they want to they can spread their wings; where men who are running farms cannot. But I find that as long as a woman has respect for a man the relationship can still work. However, some women expect such a lot. They have maybe gone to university, and feel that every man you introduce them to ought to have done the same. But so often in farming families the young men don't go on to higher education because they're expected to stay at home and work. As long as the man is bright and intelligent, and he is valued as a person, no matter how highly educated a woman she should still consider this type of man. But not everyone agrees.

One day in February I put the phone down on a client who had made me really cross. After running the Bureau for so long I don't get easily upset by people and have learned to take them for what they are. But oh, this woman!

Basically she was such a snob. She obviously felt superior to everyone else and never gave any man a chance. I'd introduced her to a man of the same age who had charisma and a mind of his own, ran his own farm and worked hard, but didn't get out and about much and didn't socialise well. First of all, she condemned the way he spoke. 'He has such an accent, and he sounds so old,' she complained.

Well, yes, he didn't speak with a plum in his mouth as she did. He lived in south

Warwickshire—but to me Warwickshire people have hardly any accent.

He had said he went to IT classes, and she thought that was so funny. I asked her what she thought was wrong with that. 'Well, it's just so laughable.' Then she added, 'I couldn't possibly meet him—whatever would my friends say?'

I certainly had to bite my tongue, because the previous month she had asked if she could pay her fees by monthly instalments. I had said yes, but isn't it ironic that someone so obviously short of money could criticise and ridicule a good, hard-working man who, although he may not have been in her class, or so she thought, could at least pay his way?

Anne, from whom I received a letter at about the same time, was a much more positive proposition and really made me feel that winter was shouting to make way for spring. She was a health visitor in her late forties, and I reckoned she was quite a daring, adaptable lady. She had told me she had flown a glider, went parachute jumping and did a lot of sailing; she had also said she could do plumbing and electrics. This had given me a clue that she must be energetic, willing to have a go at anything in life, and would definitely need a man who, like her, knew his own mind and had a strong character.

Anne's letter was about Roger, whom I had introduced to her. Roger lived in mid-Wales, a long way from Anne, and I wondered if it was feasible. But he had said he enjoyed driving steam engines and riding horses, and I liked the statement he had made on his form: 'I treat women as equals.' That was good. He also said, 'A person's status is part of the past. The future is more important.' So many countrymen don't say that. Yes, I liked this man. He was a thinker and had no prejudices.

Anne started by saying that she and Roger had been in touch. 'Roger first phoned me when I was at work and spoke to my father. I was amazed that they had had a long conversation, although Roger was very discreet and didn't reveal to my father that he'd never met me. He now tells me how difficult it was to speak to my father when he'd never met the daughter the father was talking about!'

'I knew I shouldn't reveal we'd been put together through an introduction agency,' Roger had told her. 'That was a challenge and a half with such an inquisitive father.'

'When I got in from work,' Anne's letter continued, 'I phoned him back, but he was out, so I left a message on his machine. Sure enough, the next time he phoned me I was out as well. This went on a little longer, but we had found out that we purposely didn't have mobiles—something we had in common.

'I then sent him my e-mail address and had a lovely long e-mail, full of chat and conversation and so nice to get. I immediately sent Roger an e-mail back. When he replied a few days later he'd picked up that I'd previously mentioned I had ten days' holiday from work and hadn't planned to go away anywhere.'

Roger asked if they could meet up at the start of her days off. 'I know we haven't even spoken to each other yet,' he said, 'but let's be daring and have a go. At the very worst you will only have ruined a perfectly good day if it doesn't go well—

but let's see.'

Why not, Anne thought to herself. She went on, 'I treated myself to a new outfit and had my hair done. I arrived half an hour early in the foyer of a hotel by the Severn Bridge, and amazingly I was nervous. About ten minutes before our appointed time in walked this tall, broad-shouldered man with a closely cut beard who had a great smile. Straightaway we recognised each other, and he came up and gave me a little peck on the cheek. I liked the fact that he was warm and confident enough to do that. He asked if I'd like coffee and ordered some straightaway. I liked that—he was decisive and took matters in hand.

'We sat down and started to talk. He seemed interested in my journey, in me generally, although he didn't bombard me with questions. He seemed to have an inquiring mind—and he wouldn't let me pay for the drink. We were sitting in these comfortable deep leather chairs, and I felt so relaxed with this man whom I'd only met ten minutes before. When the conversation slowed down a little he started to smile at me and say how very attractive I was and what a pleasure it was to be in my company.

'I smiled back and he looked at me and said, "It's good, isn't it?"

' "Yes," I replied. I knew what he meant. We felt so calm together, and although we hardly knew anything about each other we felt we knew everything. I couldn't believe it. Roger then suggested that we drive a little and have lunch in a country pub. I'd parked my car in the corner of the hotel car park, so I knew it would be all right and accepted his invitation.

'He had an old Range Rover, just right for this unpretentious man who had the car because it suited him and not to show off. Roger said he had actually seen a very nice place to eat at Caerleon, just a little way back over the bridge. Would I like to go there? In all honesty I wasn't bothered where I went. I was just enjoying so much being with this man and sitting close to him in the car—I could smell his freshness and masculinity.

'Lunch was just right. We sat across the table from each other and on several occasions actually started to look into each other's eyes for short moments. This was going so well it was a bit scary.

'We learned we had two children each, who were about the same ages. We discovered we liked the same music, read the same daily paper and enjoyed the same books. Although he lives in Wales Roger isn't Welsh, and amazingly we found that our families come from the same small area of Scotland. I lived in that area until my early twenties, but Roger's parents moved away to Wales when he was a year old. He took over the family farm when his father retired two years ago, and before that he developed his own business.

'After lunch, as we walked out to the car, I was still asking questions about his farm.

' "Where would you like to go now?" he asked.

' "Don't mind," was my reply.

'He turned round and said, "Would you like to come and see the farm?"

'Without further thought I immediately said I would.

'I have to report back to you, Pat, that I didn't return from his farm for a week. So I think you can draw your own conclusions as to the affection, affinity, compatibility and love we found we had together right from the start. Once we had fallen into each other's arms we couldn't draw ourselves apart. It was magic, and I honestly have to say I have never felt such overwhelming closeness with someone before.

'I have already given in my notice to the Health Authority and applied for a position in Roger's area. We're planning for me to move in permanently with him as soon as I can. He is everything I could ever have wished for in a partner, and truly he is my soulmate.'

Enclosed was a photograph of them both, looking exactly as I'd imagined them. Both good-looking, mature yet full of life, arms around each other and looking into each other's eyes.

'Oh! Isn't it lovely!' I said out loud, and shouted 'Yes, yes, yes!' and threw both arms in the air for joy.

But back to work. Even if Roger and Anne were in their seventh heaven other people were still coming to me in the hope of meeting someone special, and one man who came around that time was Tom. My first impression was of a very tall, slim man with wavy blond hair. Although in his early fifties, he certainly didn't look that old. He had been born and brought up on the farm where he still lived, close to Halesworth in Suffolk, and spoke in a lilting East Anglian dialect, not so strong that you couldn't understand him but broad enough to be distinctive. He was obviously a quiet man as I had a dreadful job at first to get him to answer more than a single word to any of my questions, but he did reveal that it had been a very big decision on his part to come over to Derbyshire as he rarely drove long distances or travelled about the countryside.

Becoming a little more expansive as we got the measure of each other Tom described his early years, which were mostly made up of work, work and more work. In his twenties he had married his first girlfriend, a good farmer's daughter, and it was as satisfactory as most marriages. She worked hard on the farm in the early years, and when he was thirty and she was twenty-two they had their first child. He added, 'We didn't plan it, but eventually we had seven children. They are now twenty-one, nineteen, sixteen, thirteen, ten, seven and five.'

Then he described his disbelief and utter shock when three years ago his wife had told him that there was someone else in her life and she was going to leave him. Unusually in a marriage break-up, however, all the children said they wanted to stop at the farm and continue living with their father. The farm was their home, and that's where they wanted to be. The little ones didn't understand or have a say in the matter, of course, but the older children were adamant they did not want to be parted from each other. The two oldest, having left school, took turns to help their dad look after the two youngest until they went to nursery school.

It was tough to start with. But after a while things got easier when their mother (by then his ex-wife) suggested that she should come to the house most days to cook and clean, and Tom readily agreed. It would mean the house would be kept tidy, the children would be looked after when they came home from nursery and school, and he would get a cooked meal once a day.

I asked if she still did all this.

'Yes, every day she comes in for an hour or two.'

I immediately pointed out that this would be a very difficult situation for any other woman to accept.

'I know,' he replied, adding that he could not alter the situation at the moment because he depended on her so much.

When I got to know him better, as he sat in front of me I could see the lovely warmth in his nature; indeed, he admitted that he hated conflict or arguments. He had never had much time for hobbies, since farm and family had always taken up his every available moment. But in his youth he had enjoyed driving in motor rallies, and now, in his fifties, he would occasionally go and watch local motor events. He really felt that he should only meet a farming lady—someone whom he could talk to about farming. I felt this was possibly to some extent because he didn't converse easily, and I knew that at least he would be able to get a conversation going with someone if he could talk about sheep!

His first introduction was to a lady a little younger than himself who, when they met, gave him a cake she had baked that day. His first response was to say his ex-wife also made very good cakes. This lady was put off right from the start, and she told me she didn't wish to meet Tom again because of his remarks. I apologised on his behalf and immediately got on the phone to tell him what a silly response he had given her. The last thing any woman wants is to be judged alongside an ex-wife, especially face to face and

173

over some domestic matter such as a home-made cake.

Tom took this all in, apologised for his comments and said he hoped he could have another introduction soon. He promised me he would be very careful about what he said to the next one.

Jennifer, in her early fifties, joined the Bureau a month or two later and very quickly I thought of Tom. She lived in Beccles, not too far away. And she was definitely involved in farming. In fact Jennifer raised pedigree stock on her own land, some of which she had let out since the death of her husband. Most of all she wanted to meet a farmer whom she hoped would not live too far from her.

When I asked Jennifer what had made her come to my Bureau, she replied, 'My husband died and I just felt so very lonely. I love people—hate being on my own. And I never had children, so when I was widowed I didn't even have a family to turn to.'

She was obviously a straightforward lady and I decided they could definitely be a good match, but of course you never know. When I first mentioned Tom to Jennifer I warned her, 'Hold your breath— he has seven children at home living with him.'

There was complete silence. Eventually she came round from the shock and said, 'Really? Well, I've always wanted to be part of a big family, but I was never able to have children of my own. Maybe this is what I'm destined for.'

'Another thing to take in, Jennifer,' I went on to say, 'is that the ex-wife still comes in every day to cook and clean.'

Another silence, then, 'Well, good for her. At least if her children aren't with her she's making sure they're fed well and the house is looked after.'

What a good, sensible woman this is, I said to myself. Shortly afterwards I introduced them and asked Tom to get in touch with Jennifer.

Very quickly Jennifer got back to me and said, 'He's a man with many good points and one of those is patience.'

When Tom phoned her to make their first contact it was quite a brief call. They found they could talk easily about farming issues, and for shy Tom it was good to be able to get the conversation going by talking about lamb prices. They spoke about six times before they met: Jennifer was going to cattle shows all over the country in those early weekends, so they just couldn't get together. For their first meeting Tom travelled about three-quarters of the way, but Jennifer could only stay for an hour as she had promised to help at a village market.

'I was struck by his height and broad shoulders, and he did look gorgeous,' she said, recalling to me the moment when she first saw him. That hour was good enough to encourage them both. And very soon Jennifer said, 'That's the man for me.'

'What made the decision for you?' I asked when she was telling me their story.

'I've got a good idea of people. What you saw was what you got—he was shy and gentle, and the gentle part was so important. The situation at home for Tom was difficult. He wanted to show me the farm, but his ex-wife was always there.' Jennifer described how, the first time he asked her to join him on the farm, he met her in the top field

175

in the dirtiest muck-spreader you could imagine. It was filthy and old, and to cap it all Tom had cow muck all across one side of his glasses. When the muck spreading was finished he walked her around the fields on his big long legs, leaving her miles behind as she struggled to keep up with him.

For the next few meetings she joined him in the fields on whatever job he was doing, usually on a tractor, but wouldn't go down to the farmhouse. 'The most difficult aspect was that his ex-wife still kept coming round to look after the children. Sometimes she would come twice a day, once to do the house up and later to cook their dinner. But one day I'd been helping Tom outside and he said, "Come on, I want to introduce you to my ex-wife."

'I was so nervous, but amazingly she was nice and even made me a cup of tea. Then more progress was made in that I met some of the children, and within a fortnight I'd seen them all. Such lovely children, all very nice and well-mannered. They're a credit to Tom—they're all right.

'Over this time we got to know each other more and I got to know the children. What I liked is that every evening after dinner they all sat in the farmhouse kitchen and talked over how each of them had spent their day. It was such a lovely family atmosphere.

'One day Tom and I decided to go up to Scotland for some cattle sales. It was unusual for him to have time off and travel such a long distance. It was there that we spent some lovely quiet days together and shared our nights, and it was there that we decided to get engaged.

'When we got home Tom got all the children in

the kitchen and told them we had got engaged to be married and showed them my ring. There was a hushed silence—they were utterly astounded that their dad could do anything like that. The next day he told his ex-wife about our plans and she too was totally shocked, but then congratulated us and meekly went away.'

Slowly over the next few days congratulations cards were given to them by each child. Most of it was apparently organised by the eldest girl. Then Tom decided it was about time his ex-wife stopped coming to the farm routinely. He told her she could only come occasionally to see the children, and that had to be by prior arrangement. That didn't go down well, Jennifer told me, but Tom's mother was still alive and said he was doing the right thing. Thankfully, Jennifer got on well with his mother.

She went on, 'I decided I wanted Tom to meet my family, but he felt he should first buy some new clothes—he hadn't bothered with this side of his life for years. So we went and got him a new outfit, and he was introduced to my extended family at a little party I gave to announce our engagement. They all liked him so much. "A little quiet but salt of the earth" was the general comment.

'I now go most days and prepare a meal for the seven children and Tom and myself. I clean the house, but the kids are very good and do a lot for themselves, especially the older ones. We're now planning our small wedding, and we'll have a blessing afterwards in the little church in the grounds of the farm. The children seem to be getting excited, and the two little girls of seven and five are going to be bridesmaids.

'Also, a lot of talk is taking place with the older children as Tom wants to encourage them to take over running the farm in about three to five years' time. We want to spend a lot of years together without Tom working from morning to night. We think that, if I keep my house, it will be just right for us to move back into when he retires and the children take over. Now we are counting the days to our wedding, and then I can start a full role as wife and stepmother of these seven lovely children.'

What a wonderful outcome. Around this time I also heard news of a rather different relationship, being conducted not in a very full farmhouse but thousands of miles apart.

Over the months Yvonne had called me regularly, telling me about herself and Tony—who had gone to Africa for six months—and how they were getting on. Apparently they spoke two or three times a week on his satellite phone. She said she was really beginning to know him well and was so amused that she could hear real jungle sounds in the background when he spoke to her. Then one day she phoned me and couldn't stop laughing about an incident concerning Tony which had, she said, a funny side.

'Whatever is the joke?' I asked.

'Well, it's not actually a joke and maybe it's a bit sick of me to laugh, but I can just see the sketch on TV,' she said. 'The thing is, Tony has just phoned me and described the predicament he was in—as he said, "I think it's about time you knew my impediment."' At this, Yvonne was somewhat nonplussed. "The fact is," Tony went on, "I'm sitting on a bridge which goes over this fast-running river and part of my artificial leg has just dropped on to the bank by the side of the river."

Yvonne told me, 'I was speechless—I really didn't know that he had an artificial leg. But then I laughed as I could see the funny side of it all. He went on to say that he hadn't wanted to tell me immediately about his leg in case it put me off him. Then whenever he thought about saying something it didn't seem to be the right time. But while he was sitting there waiting for someone to retrieve his "part" for him he realised this was the right time to just throw caution to the wind and tell me.'

We both laughed, and she added that his leg didn't bother her at all—she was just amazed that she hadn't detected it on their two meetings. I told her that I very often have someone with a false eye join the agency—farmers are prone to accidents. My last experience of this had been when a woman had obviously got one, but hadn't told the man or me before she met him. He later got on the phone to ask me to tell her he didn't want to see her again because of the eye. That was a very difficult thing to do, and I have to admit I made up some other excuse. Women don't seem so concerned if they meet a man with this kind of difficulty.

Yvonne's daughter, who had planned to go out to Africa, did so but never met up with Tony. It's a big continent but what a shame—I think Yvonne had visions of her daughter and Tony striding through the jungle to meet up accidentally like Stanley and Livingstone.

Sadly, when Tony later returned to Britain, Yvonne found he could show no physical warmth and found it difficult to understand her feminine side. They parted amicably after several months of

179

trying to understand each other but not succeeding.

Yvonne is a lovely lady and I am so pleased to call her a good friend, but she doesn't seem to have much luck with men. Another man I introduced her to, the nicest and kindest of men on this earth who certainly would have understood her feminine side, was Donald. Eventually, after a few months of getting to know each other, they went on holiday with her three children to Cornwall. This trip was supposed to have introduced Donald to her family and enabled the children to get to know him. It was a disaster. The children were all at different universities, so when they met up after several months apart they just wanted to talk and talk—but only to each other. Donald felt very left out of things, Yvonne tried to bring them all together, but eventually it fell apart and they went their separate ways. To date not Yvonne, nor Donald nor Tony has met anyone who is special for them, but Yvonne and I often recall Tony and his false leg and laugh about it.

On that day in 2001 when she called me I went on to tell her about two men who had recently phoned me up. I'd introduced one young man to a woman in her thirties. They had both been through a divorce rather early in adult life, and didn't live too far apart. She was a farmer's daughter, and he was a livestock farmer from Leicestershire. His photo showed a rather good-looking, blond man reminiscent of the young Robert Redford. One evening he telephoned me to say, 'She's so damn nice, she's too good for me.'

'What do you mean,' was my instant reply.

'She's perfect in every way, but I think I'm a

rogue and I know I don't treat women too well. I mean I've never physically hurt a woman, but I know what I'm like. I wouldn't consider her like I should, I'd fail to turn up when she'd be expecting me to, I'd get drunk when I shouldn't. All in all, I've really thought about it and I know I can't do this to such a lovely girl. So because she's too nice I want to give her up. I would break her heart.'

That was a first in all my years of matchmaking.

The next request was made in broad dialect by a man who stated in the gruffest way imaginable, 'Well, Mrs Warren, I don't want a rough woman, you know. Me mother says we want a bit of culture brought into this family.' She was probably right. Then I thought of an old saying: a mother hopes her daughter will get a better husband than she did, but she knows her son will never get a better wife than his father did.

I love to hear from old friends, and one morning I had a most rewarding telephone call from Iris. Mark had asked my advice a short while before about how to go about asking her to marry him.

'Be conventional and romantic,' I'd said. Women love that.

Iris started by telling me they'd spent a fortnight in Mexico together and had never had a cross word.

'Good God! That's something John and I have never accomplished,' I laughingly told her.

'Guess what?' she went on.

'I wouldn't know, Iris,' I replied. 'You tell me.'

'Mark proposed one evening when we were sitting in the marriage gazebo at the hotel.'

I had known he was going to do so, of course, but didn't let on.

She continued, 'He's bought me this beautiful three-diamond ring, and he actually went down on one knee and asked me.'

I remembered that, when he'd asked my advice, I'd suggested he do just that. At the time it was lovely for me as a middle-aged woman to fantasise about how I'd like it all to happen—and he really did take in what I'd said and carried it out to the letter.

'He even telephoned my father just before the holiday and asked his permission. How about that!' added Iris.

'Oh! How wonderful,' I said with as much surprise as I could muster, and kept repeating, 'It's wonderful . . . it's wonderful . . . I'm so delighted for you both.' I was really elated, and genuinely very pleased for them. This was one wedding I knew I would very much enjoy.

That morning in the office ended by George phoning me. He was the lovely old man of eighty who had come to see me a few months back and had brought me fresh vegetables from his garden. I'd told him it would be very difficult to find a good introduction because of his age, but that I would try.

While he was with me at the interview I'd thought of Nancy, and had told him about her. He'd said he was very interested, but deep down I was quite sceptical about it all. Afterwards I contacted Nancy, who was delighted to hear about George and readily accepted an introduction to him. I'd not heard from either of them since.

'I just thought I'd tell you everything is going very well,' said George on the phone. 'I've spent many weekends there at her cottage and our days are so good together. We go out, and Nancy invites her friends over. We seem to be enjoying every moment.'

I was truly amazed, and ashamed at all my negativity. Love, in all its forms, is truly a many-splendoured thing.

CHAPTER FOURTEEN

SEX ALL MORNING

Sometimes a matchmaker's duties can be incredibly straightforward and achieve quick results—it's a kind of quick-fix gratification and can be very welcome. For instance, one of my successful Bureau members had come to tell me about the lovely life she and the man I'd introduced her to were having, then mentioned her son and the name of the girlfriend he'd had until recently. I said that I knew the girl personally and she did seem very nice. We were both surprised that we appeared to live in such a small world, but I'd happened to meet her though her parents. The mother, upset that this agreeable girl was no longer with her son, said that he had acted very foolishly and she understood why the relationship had broken down. Then she had an idea: what if I could ask her if she would give him a second chance?

'I'll do that willingly,' I said. 'But if she says no you must accept it.'

'Yes, of course,' said the mother. 'I don't want to ask her personally—we always got on so well that I think she would find it difficult to say no to my face. But you aren't so close to her as me.'

So I asked her and she didn't say no—in fact she was terribly pleased he wanted her back. Soon they were dating again and all was going well. The mother was delighted, and it was lovely to be able to do something so simple that made everyone

184

happy.

But they aren't all as easy as that. The next day when I'd finished my morning in the office I dragged myself into the kitchen and realised how tired I was.

'What's the matter?' asked John.

'I've had sex all morning,' I replied. 'I'm exhausted!' And it was true—I really wasn't able to do anything else for a few minutes because my mind was in such a whirl. I'm a pretty tough character, but I was exhausted because of this three-letter word.

It had been one of those rare mornings when sex had been the constant topic of conversation. For weeks on end the subject won't be mentioned at all, or perhaps someone will be very daring and enquire, 'Do you think I should kiss her goodnight on the first date?' But this morning I got one after the other asking for advice—quite explicit advice. The problem is, I'm no expert. I just use common sense and an understanding of how very important sex is to most relationships.

Bob phoned me first and said that after eighteen months of going out with Mary he had told her the evening before that he wished to end their relationship. He loved Mary very much but felt concerned that the physical side had not progressed any further. I asked him if they had ever made love.

'No,' he said. 'We've shared a bed and we're affectionate, but we've never been fully intimate.'

I said I was very surprised that since they'd got that far, after such a long time they hadn't gone any further. Most men wouldn't have been as patient as he had. Then I asked him if he had explained how he felt to Mary before telling her he wanted to end things.

'No, no, I haven't,' he replied.

'But why not?' I asked in amazement.

'I just couldn't bring myself to—I just couldn't.'

'Well, what reason did you give her for breaking it off?' I asked.

'I said I felt she wasn't as committed as I was, and therefore I didn't want to continue.'

Within half an hour of Bob putting the phone down Mary called me. She seemed devastated that Bob no longer wished to see her and didn't understand why. She wanted to know what I thought.

I didn't feel I should reveal that Bob had just called me—let alone that he had talked through it all with me. So I just asked her to think hard. There must have been a reason somewhere. I suggested that if someone wished to move on after eighteen months it might be because something in their relationship wasn't fulfilling all their expectations—what did she think that could be?

Mary thought for a while, then said that their relationship hadn't been fully intimate and maybe it was because of that.

I said I thought she was right, and that I felt she had to make a choice. She could face the fact that she didn't feel sex was as important in a relationship as Bob did, if that were so, in which case they were incompatible in this area and maybe it would be best to part. Or she needed virtually to seduce him in the next few days and demonstrate her desire to love him more. I suggested that if she went down this avenue she should arrange a spur-of-the-moment holiday on which they could relax and see where it would lead.

She said she would think about it. Within the hour she was on the phone again to me, saying she had given it serious thought and was now willing to enter into a full sexual relationship with him. However, she felt she couldn't tell him herself. Would I do it for her?

'It would be much better coming from you, Mary, really it would.'

'No, no. *Please* would you telephone him, Pat, and tell him?'

So I dialled Bob's number once again and I explained my mission. I told him Mary had spoken to me and was dreadfully upset at what he had said about ending their relationship. She had thought things through and decided that, if it was bothering him that they had not made love, she would throw caution to the wind and enter into full intimacy.

'It's too late,' he said. 'If she'd loved me enough she'd have wanted that before.'

I did tend to agree with him, but I didn't let on. 'Give her another chance, Bob,' I implored, but he said he still thought he didn't want to go back on his decision.

Once again I spoke to Mary and had to report my conversation with Bob.

She was devastated. 'I know how wrong I've been, and I want to put it all right,' she said tearfully.

'Right,' I said. 'I think you've got to be the positive one here, Mary. No shilly-shallying—you've got to go out and get this man. Meet up with him and do something very different—you need to get his attention, to make him realise you've changed and that you want him to know that. Be bold—be the pursuer. You may not succeed in catching him, but if you feel he's worth fighting for you must do your best.'

She came off the phone saying how wonderfully positive she would make herself, and that she was determined to go out and make it obvious to Bob that she wanted him in all ways.

Immediately I'd finished this call the phone rang again, but this time I was in for a little surprise.

'This is Radio Derby. Did you know, Patricia, it's National Flirting Day?'

'Well, that's very nice,' I said. 'Is it?'

'Yes, and what we want you to do straightaway is talk to our audience now about flirting.'

'What? Now? Straight away?' I asked.

'Yes, you're live in two seconds.'

I took a deep gulp. I know nothing about flirting. Hell's bells—you associate flirting with teenage girls and here I was in my mid-fifties. I couldn't let the audience know my age. Flirting wouldn't fit comfortably with the image of me as an oldish lady. Then I was live and on the air.

'Tell us how to flirt,' demanded the two interviewers, one male and one female, after they had introduced me.

Quickly I went back to being sixteen years old and described how I would flirt with my boyfriend Johnny at school.

'Look them straight in the eye,' I said. 'Make them feel you are totally and absolutely interested in them and them alone. Be very smiley and happy, carefree and light-hearted. Be intriguing and understanding, but keep it light all the time. Joke and make them feel you are completely interested in them above anyone else in the world.'

Then a bit of light-hearted banter took place and the man said, 'Can you feel I'm trying to flirt with you, Patricia?'

Well, I couldn't at all—but I had to keep my end up so I uttered a few silly words and said it was difficult to detect that over the phone but it seemed very complimentary if he was. This was starting to be hell—*Get me off this live radio*, I thought. At last, with giggles all around (even from me), they thanked me for speaking to their audience and I said goodbye to them all.

Thank God for that, I thought. *Let me just get on with my work.*

Head down, I started to type out a profile when the phone rang again and this time it was Susan, a girl who I knew had fallen in love after several months with her last introduction.

'I need your advice, Pat. Sam and I are so in love and I adore going over to his farm. His father lives with him, you know. We've known each other for nearly eight months now and I love him so much. When I go over he wants to come to the guest bedroom where I sleep. It's wonderful to lie with him and for us to be together, but I just can't make love because his father's bedroom is next door. And Sam's bedroom is the other side of his father's—so wherever we are I dread the thought that his father would hear us.'

Oh dear, for how many centuries has this dilemma been going on? I thought. I would have liked to have said, 'You've both waited so long for this—you're both in your late thirties, not young and immature. You've both never had such a good relationship before—enjoy it.' But I knew that wouldn't be the definitive answer, so I said that

189

quite honestly I didn't know what to suggest.

Finally that morning William rang and said he'd got on so well with Sally, to whom I'd introduced him, but that he was so upset because he was impotent. 'I'm sixty-seven, you know.'

After all the goings on that morning, quite honestly I'd had enough. I told him emphatically that I understood there were now many products on the market to help him overcome this problem and that just a few minutes with his doctor would put things right.

Wow! I can't take any more, I thought.

I left the office feeling I really deserved the short break I had planned for the next few days, staying with my good friend Maria who lives in the south. About twelve years previously she had needed a helping hand. She had no one she could turn to for advice and who would give her the necessary confidence to leave the family she was working for, who were treating her very badly. I helped her take that next step in life and she has progressed into a successful businesswoman who now owns a residential nursing home.

I think it was on my second day staying with Maria that I had a desperate phone call from John. 'Have you heard the news?'

'No. What am I supposed to have heard?' I replied.

'Foot and mouth has been reported—it's terrible. It will affect everyone in farming. Whatever will happen to us? It will affect our herd. We won't be able to have the sale.'

CHAPTER FIFTEEN

FOOT AND MOUTH

The power of the human spirit was certainly put to the test in the agricultural world in the early spring of 2001, when foot and mouth disease was diagnosed in many parts of the country. Some Bureau members who were in the middle of the whole awful business went completely quiet for weeks. They couldn't venture off their farms, their stock had been killed and they were in such shock that they couldn't raise their heads to deal with another day. Some of those who were affected by foot and mouth told me that they literally went to bed for days. They couldn't accept that all their animals had been culled, especially if the animals didn't have the disease but were just contacts. Of course, the men on my register were usually living by themselves, with no wife or girlfriend for support. To some I became that much-needed crutch, and from time to time grown men wept uncontrollably down the phone. I would just listen and then try very hard to get them to look to the future. I felt at least I had done my bit, however small, to help with this dreadful episode in farming life.

Gradually, as the year progressed from those awful early days in February and March, spring arrived, things started to get a little back to normal, and of course life had to go on. Foot and mouth continued all summer, but we tried to develop an optimistic outlook on life.

191

At the beginning of May Iris asked me to look at two churches where she and Mark might hold their wedding. I travelled down to Mark's farm, and spent some time being shown around his enormous Georgian farmhouse crammed full of spectacular antiques. Iris showed me the little church a few yards down the road—rarely used, and full of dust. The next day I walked round Iris's village church in Derbyshire, and instantly we both felt that the wedding would be better there.

Once the church had been agreed, Mark phoned to ask me to suggest some possible reception venues in the area. I suggested my favourite hotel, and he then asked me to accompany him and Iris there for lunch to try it out. We did, it was great, and amazingly they'd got the appropriate date free. So the reception was booked and I sat back with a huge grin of satisfaction.

Maybe nothing really worthwhile in life comes that easy, because about two weeks after that I got a telephone call from Iris asking me to go and see her.

'I can't go through with it, I just can't!' she cried out.

'Whatever is the matter?' I said in astonishment.

'It's just too much for me—everyone, my dad and Mark's dad, they all want this big wedding. I'm not that sort of person, and I know Mark feels the same. I just wanted a quiet affair. I really just want Mark and me to be together, and I don't want all this stress.'

'This is *your* life, Iris—be strong and tell them all. Don't do what everyone says you have to do. Be brave and stand up for yourself.' Such were my words of advice, and I felt anyone would have said

192

the same.

So Iris and Mark's wedding was cancelled. Mark took matters in hand, as he understood how she felt, and spoke to the vicar and the hotel. The honeymoon to Morocco, however, was not cancelled—they were to turn that into a holiday, and duly went on the supposed honeymoon but without having gone through the stress of a wedding.

On their return Mark decided very quickly to buy a lovely house for himself and Iris in a village near his farm. *What a great solution*, I thought. No comparisons to his mother's housekeeping—Iris's old fear—there. It would be a brand-new life for Iris and also for him, away from his farm for the first time ever—Mark had been born at his farmhouse and had never lived anywhere else. His father, however, would still be there to keep an eye on things. But the two of them, Mark and Iris, were just going to enjoy experiencing a new life and being together.

As they made plans to move in together and start to live their lives with a partner, which they had wanted for so long, it was both exciting and worrying.

'Do you think we'll be all right?' Iris asked me. 'I'm frightened to death.'

'Yes, you will be, Iris. You'll find it difficult, both of you, at times. Even people who have lived together twenty years do. But you'll never get there if you don't try it. To get anything you want in life you have to be courageous and grab your happiness with both hands,' I urged her.

Both in their forties and never done it before. I wished them all the happiness in the world.

Back at our Farm, as the 22nd of May approached the most important thing on our minds was what we were going to do about our dairy herd. Even though the auctioneers had fixed the sale date the previous autumn, we couldn't sell them in the ring due to foot and mouth restrictions. John said he had read that some of the early farms affected by foot and mouth were now thinking about restocking. If we couldn't sell by auction, maybe we could do so privately, on a one-to-one basis. So, not knowing if it would work, we set to and advertised our herd in the *Farmer's Guardian* newspaper.

In the following weeks some six farmers phoned and said they were interested because all their cows had been slaughtered because of foot and mouth. To each we sent full details of the herd's breeding and milk production, and they all said they wanted to come and see them. They couldn't visit us, of course, until their farms had been thoroughly cleaned. Two of those families soon realised it would take months for that procedure to be finalised and therefore they couldn't consider buying another herd so soon. Another couple weren't prepared to adhere to the rules laid down by the Ministry, DEFRA (or to give it its full long-winded title, the Department for Environment, Food and Rural Affairs). Those rules were that, even after your own farm had been cleaned, if you visited a non-contaminated farm in an area of the country that had never been affected you had first to live in a non-farming situation—a town or city—for three days.

In the end only three families seemed willing to do all this to come and take a look at our herd.

DEFRA insisted that we supply each visitor with brand-new overalls and wellingtons, all to be left with us afterwards. It cost us a fortune, and on top of that they had to park their cars in the village and be collected from there by us.

So these three potential buyers, on separate occasions after holidaying in Sheffield or Derby for three consecutive days, came to visit us. All were nice, but we took a special liking to the last couple that came. Gordon and Fiona were from Scotland. They were very unassuming people but obviously successful in what they did and determined that foot and mouth would not deter them from their great love, farming. Their story of what they had gone through would be similar to that of thousands of others—possibly the most harrowing and traumatic situation they would ever face.

They had not actually had foot and mouth, but their neighbour had. They saw no evidence of the disease in any of their cattle and sheep, yet every one of them had to be slaughtered. They told us that one Saturday morning they woke up full of optimism that it would not happen to them. They'd done their early morning check of their animals and everything was well—they were definitely all fit and healthy. Then at nine o'clock that morning they had a call to say that all their dairy and beef stock were to be killed immediately as their neighbour's stock had foot and mouth. The sheep apparently would be done later. They were completely devastated—there was no appeal, and they had no say in the matter. One phone call, and their whole life had been torn to shreds.

By 11 a.m. five slaughtermen had arrived. They were big strong men who carried huge knives in their belts; they told Gordon and Fiona that they would be killing the stock with guns, but that afterwards they would have to slit the cows' throats. They turned out to be good men, just doing their jobs, grateful for any understanding and very gentlemanly to Fiona. They told her they would not have a woman in the slaughter sheds with them, so she and Gordon retreated to their house—Gordon said he could not face it alone. An organised caterer arrived with bacon sandwiches and coffee for the men, and some was taken to them in the farmhouse. But of course they couldn't face eating at a time like that. When it had all finished, the blood from over two hundred head of stock was running everywhere.

It seemed such a strange thing that out of nowhere, but obviously all prearranged, a fish supper was brought to them at 8 p.m. Exactly on the dot of when the five slaughtermen finished work for the day.

The most horrific time was yet to come, and that was the days of waiting until their dead cows were collected. This did not happen until the Wednesday and Thursday: for four or five days they had to wait, with blood everywhere and the stench gaining strength every day, and stare at huge piles of bloated carcasses which had once been their beautiful cattle which they had bred, loved and nurtured.

They did eventually sleep a little through sheer exhaustion. For the first time in Gordon's life he woke up on a Sunday with absolutely nothing to do. They had sheep that they should attend to at their other farm, but as that was some miles away they were not allowed to go to them. Then on the

Monday they were told that the Army would pick them up to take them out to their sheep—but only because all of those were to be shot too. They protested vehemently. The sheep were away at another farm and not close to any outbreaks. But once again no appeal was considered: according to DEFRA they had no say in the matter and no rights.

Waiting to be picked up by the Army seemed to turn this whole affair into a surrealist nightmare in a police state, they said. It turned out the soldiers had no idea about animals, unlike the slaughtermen who worked with them every day. Once the shooting began some of the soldiers started to be sick, and that continued all day.

That evening, when they returned home in the Army lorries, they stood at the door and saw five separate fires in the surrounding countryside where other cattle carcasses were being burnt. But they could hardly breathe due to the stench of their own dead cows, which still had not been burnt or taken away. Seagulls were on the bodies pulling away the flesh and flying off—it seemed to Gordon and Fiona that they had somehow arrived in hell.

Neighbours going through the same experience said later they were so traumatised that they couldn't talk to anyone who wasn't going through it themselves, because they just couldn't understand. There seemed no point in trying to talk about the depths of despair they had reached. Gordon and Fiona told us they really just went into themselves—they couldn't leave the farm for any purpose, and didn't want to. Groceries were left by friends at the end of the drive—not that they looked forward to their food. For two full weeks they just sat around the house, slept a little, talked some but mostly cried.

The turning point came when all the cows had been loaded on to lorries and taken away, and they realised they had moved on to another phase in their lives. They wanted to be doing, they were used to working, and felt they would literally go mad if they didn't start rolling up their sleeves again and getting on with things. After much insistence on their part they were told that they could start washing out the farm. There was dried blood everywhere, and the family started by power hosing all the surfaces. It was an immense job on a large farm of 1000 acres with buildings to match, and they just buried themselves in the therapy of work. After the power hosing they had to use a degreasing substance over all the buildings, which was then power hosed off again. Then everywhere was disinfected.

Eventually the farm was deemed to be clean. Then they started thinking about restocking. They saw our advert quite by chance and realised they'd like to buy our herd. For three days, as per the rules, they stayed at a hotel in Derby. On their visit to us we picked them up from the village and they put on the new boiler suits and wellingtons. They inspected the whole herd for several hours, had tea with us and promptly set off on their journey back up to Scotland. They promised to phone once they got home, which they did. On the way back they had decided to make us an offer for the herd, which they did that day. We accepted on the following day and immediately we wrote out a sale document. We sent them a copy, which they signed in the presence of their bank manager as a witness and then returned to us. We signed ours likewise and sent it to them.

Both parties deemed that we had a contract which would secure the purchase of the cows for them and a good sale for us. But they couldn't yet take possession of the herd as no licences were being issued to transport animals anywhere in the UK. So the deal was that we would keep the herd for the time being and treat them as if they were our own, and sell the milk, but of course not sell them to anyone else. We were pleased with this arrangement. Gordon and Fiona gave us a hefty deposit for the cows, and we knew we could look forward to the balance in due course.

With that matter settled, John and I paid attention to other things. John turned to the running of the farm, and I applied my energies once again to the Bureau. But just occasionally in that bizarre, cruel year there were moments of pleasure.

As we got into the middle of June, Midsummer Day approached. Being so close to Arbor Low, I always get the urge at this time to join in the summer solstice celebrations and watch the sun rise from this ancient stone circle. It's very often cloudy and you can't actually see that red ball slowly rising from behind the distant hills, but a sense of mystery and the spirit of our ancestors still hover around this place. My friend Jill, who is really quite adventurous as she has travelled all over the world by herself, said she would love to come too. At 3 a.m. I drove down and picked her up from the village, and then we slipped quietly back through the sleeping houses.

As we drove up the hill, with the headlights picking out the heavy green summer foliage of elder bushes and the great froths of cow parsley on either side of the road, we could almost hear the countryside breathing with the warmth and lush growth. When we got back to the farm I drove as far as I could, after which we would have three fields to cross on foot—I couldn't take the four-wheel drive as the grass was high, ready for cutting. Luckily there were no cows about, because Jill is terrified of them. In fact, when she visits the farm John or I have to fetch her by car from the gate at the end of the drive, because she daren't cross the field. And yet she loves everything else about the country.

We set off from the car just as the sky was beginning to lighten to a pearly grey. I had packed some bacon sandwiches and a flask of coffee—always such a treat when you're outdoors early in the morning. Knowing there would be a heavy dew I had put on wellies, but in the dark I seemed to have managed to put on John's by mistake (not for the first time), so my rather smaller feet were slopping around inside them. Jill only had trainers, so her feet were wet through in minutes.

We went through the gate into the second field and straight into waist-high grass waiting to be mown. Jill said she thought we should go round the edge but I said two ladies and a rucksack wouldn't squash much grass—and besides, the sky was growing lighter by the minute. Halfway across the field, though, I started to feel very tired. Wading through wet grass before dawn is very hard on the calf muscles, and John's wellies kept pulling my feet down and threatening to slide off altogether. I

200

could hear Jill's trainers squelching, too. I was beginning to think that perhaps I was getting too old for this sort of thing when the gate loomed into sight and I lurched thankfully towards it. I held it open for Jill, then realised she was going in a different direction—she is very short-sighted.

'Hey, Jill, where are you going?' I yelled.

She turned round, startled. 'Oh, I thought you were that hawthorn bush, Pat. It's just like you—short and round and loves being in the country.'

After this back-handed compliment she offered to carry the rucksack, which was a help. It was also a relief to see the silhouette of the stone circle not too far off and hear the voices of other people as mad as us—getting out of a cosy bed before dawn, traipsing through wet grass, just to look at a very cloudy grey horizon and pretend we could see the sun. But when I'd got my breath back, and thought of the hot coffee, I felt it was really quite a good adventure to be having.

The exit to the last field was through a stile, although it's actually more of a low wall with a step. I'm quite a short person, and what with John's wellies and the effort of wading through the grass I found that when I'd got one leg over the other wouldn't follow—I was straddled across the wall!

Jill stumbled into view, peering through the mist. 'Why are you sitting on the wall, Pat?' she panted. 'Shouldn't we be getting a move on?'

Anyway, when she realised I was stuck she couldn't stop laughing. She tried to bend over to grab my foot and hoist my leg over, but was helpless with mirth and couldn't see what was foot and what was wall. With much huffing and puffing, eventually she heaved me over and I landed on the other side—not without an effect that lasted several days.

By now it was 4 a.m. and the sun was supposed to rise at 4.10, so we made our way to the stones. If you have ever been inside a four-thousand-year-old stone circle you will certainly have felt a presence, as though our ancestors were still there. Did they really sacrifice young virgins on these stones? I shuddered at the thought. There was a professor of biochemistry who lived in the village a few years ago, and he and some friends actually did some divining with a rod. This is the process where you walk across the ground holding a hazel twig, and if there is water or a magnetic field underground the twig is drawn forcibly down. The results were extraordinary. As they walked the perimeter of the circle, the Y-shaped hazel twig was pulled down so fiercely it took the skin off their hands. What is this force that surrounds the circle? How did it get there? How has it remained? Perhaps there are some mysteries that are better left unsolved.

With my mind wandering in the past, I was startled when a priest-like shape loomed up out of the mist. I thought for a minute he was going to grab me for the sacrificial altar (although I don't think I'm quite the sort they'd be looking for now!). But it turned out to be just an old hippie wearing a hooded anorak. What is it about anoraks that is so depressing? They are shapeless, colourless and dull. I pulled the collar of my smartish black jacket closer round me. Even with John's wellies and my hair flattened by the heavy mist, I felt more dignified than if I had been wearing an anorak. Then I noticed a crowd of hippies a distance away.

The next person I banged into was, thankfully, Jill, so we found a little knoll facing east and got out the bacon sandwiches and coffee. They tasted wonderful, and it was so good to sit down. As we were having our well-earned little picnic the sun must have slipped over the horizon behind all that cloud, because the anorak-clad hippies started chanting and raising their arms and generally behaving in a ridiculous fashion. And so, in a modest way, another Midsummer Day was born in the middle of England, all those thousands of years after the stone circle was set up to welcome it. It was satisfying to have been there; Jill and I congratulated ourselves and felt it would be a good tale to tell.

I got back to the farmhouse around 6 a.m., tired, starting to get stiff and still slightly damp with dew. There was John sitting on the back step, scratching his head and obviously wondering why his size 12 feet wouldn't go into my wellies. I sat down next to him, pushed my feet out in front of me and pointed wordlessly at the mistake. He got up slowly, pulled his wellies off my feet, asked if I'd met any interesting Stone Age people and went off to do the milking. Just then the sun broke through the clouds and I lay back on the step—then realised that I'd got another venue to go to that day. I'd decided, after much cajoling, to join a group of my women friends at Ascot that year, and today was the day.

I quickly showered, did my hair and make-up, put on my special dress and heavily laden hat, and was ready just as the car which was taking us arrived. In the first half of my day I sat next to New Age travellers, and in the second half I was at times the same distance away from the Queen. How much more diverse can you get?

CHAPTER SIXTEEN

TO EVERY THING THERE IS A SEASON

To every thing there is a season, and after many years of both of them waiting to meet someone special, it was not long before the time felt completely right for Mark and Iris to get married.

They had lived together for several months and both quickly realised that there was no going back—they had found something unique.

They decided on a small country wedding, and as I arrived on the appointed afternoon at the little church that stands in the middle of the field next to Mark's farm, I knew they had chosen perfectly.

The church was filled with local flowers, which were arranged by a lady from the village, and were discreet but very pretty. They had just fifty guests and Iris looked beautiful in a simple cream and gold satin dress. She had one small bridesmaid, and they were both carrying bouquets that matched the flowers in the church.

The vicar held a beautiful service and the church brimmed with villagers who shared the couple's joy.

They made their vows with absolute sincerity and love, and when they left the church the happy pair walked under an arch of pitchforks held by other local farmers. We all spilled out onto the lush grass of the field. Iris looked radiant and Mark looked proud and confident. It was such a beautiful wedding and exactly what the couple had hoped for. I shed a few tears of happiness as we all waved goodbye and watched them set off on their future life together.

It was getting towards the end of August. We had sold our cows, but they were still in our possession and so we were still milking them twice a day and doing all the tasks associated with a dairy herd of over two hundred. We sold the milk and kept the money received. Throughout the spring and summer of 2001 no cattle could be moved without permission, and the licence we needed to take them to their new owners in Scotland was just not being issued to anyone. At the beginning of the month both we and the new owners had tried to obtain one, but DEFRA were not budging. We spoke to the new owners virtually every other day; we liked and respected them, and soon a very good bond had been built up between us.

The news that seemed to bring darkening skies over our plans was that the Scottish agricultural department were starting to put out publicity saying that, if they assured mainland Europe that no livestock at all would be accepted across the border into Scotland from England and Wales, then Europe might start importing Scottish beef again. We were devastated at this. Gordon and Fiona could hardly take it in—maybe they wouldn't be able to have their new herd until the following summer.

Then there was a suggestion from DEFRA that if this regime was introduced it would not be before the beginning of September. We were coming up to the end of August and Gordon was waiting for his farm (which, if you recall, had never actually had foot and mouth) to be given its certificate for livestock to come back on to the land. The inspector had been out before, but Gordon and Fiona said it was obvious that he had been told to make some excuse and not allow any farms to be restocked. Their farm had had its cleanliness certificate months ago, before they even came to see us. It all seemed so obviously political. Eventually, however, the Ministry ran out of excuses, permission was given to restock and the required certificate was issued.

There was now a window of five days before the Scottish border would be closed to cattle. Could we get the relevant movement licence and put into place all the necessary arrangements needed to transport a large dairy herd hundreds of miles in just a few days?

The farm clearance certificate was given to Gordon on the Tuesday, after he had driven miles across Scotland to the relevant office in Edinburgh. On Wednesday both our families applied for the movement licence, bombarding the appropriate people with certified copies of every piece of documentation we could think of. That afternoon the precious licence was granted verbally, to great whoops of joy. It would not, however, actually be written out until the Ministry vet had been to inspect every cow. So I spent most of Wednesday afternoon on the phone arranging for him to come to our farm the next day. All farmers will know the feeling: Ministry vets are like buses—when you don't want them they are always there, and when you do you can't get one for love or money. At last one was assigned to come to us the next day.

It seemed he was with us for hours, thoroughly inspecting every cow, heifer and calf. It was a gruelling few hours for both families. They were on tenterhooks in Scotland just waiting by the phone, while down in England we said a little prayer as the vet approached each animal. By midday our herd was given the all-clear and the long-awaited movement licence was written out. But our rejoicing was dampened when we were told that before we moved the herd we would have to arrange for an inspector to accompany them to Scotland. Bloody hell! How many more hoops did we have to jump through?

I phoned Gordon and Fiona, and with the closure of the border looming ever closer they suggested that if they could arrange the transport we should try for tomorrow, Friday. It all depended upon my ability to get an inspector in time. Would I be persuasive enough?

I just wouldn't give up. I phoned numerous offices and you could tell that doing something tomorrow was just a little too quick for any government department, but I knew I had to give it my best shot. By 1 p.m., after phoning around and around for an hour, getting transferred here, there and everywhere and having so many people say no, at last I got someone to say yes, that could be arranged. I couldn't believe it, and actually wouldn't until I managed to speak to the inspector personally on his mobile—after all, it could just happen that he was having the day off to take his Aunt Agatha to the dentist.

'Well, it's a bit short notice,' he said. 'But yes, I can drive up to Scotland with your lorries tomorrow.'

I rushed to find John. We had been waiting for this for months and months. Gordon in Scotland was told immediately that all was in place at our end. Did he think he could arrange the transport in time?

'Well, I'm going to move heaven and earth,' he said, 'and I'm going to work with a transport manager I know who will help me coordinate it all. I reckon we will need at least eight arctics all ready to leave your place by 6 a.m. tomorrow, which means they've got to start driving down from Scotland late this afternoon in order to have their allotted sleep overnight.' In other words, he'd got two hours to find eight lorries of the right size, with drivers, to be on the road by 4 p.m. How he did it we shall never know—I don't think he knows himself. But by the end of Thursday afternoon all these cattle wagons were being driven down to Derbyshire.

We were all terrified something would go wrong. That afternoon I put together ten document packs, containing copies of all the certificates and licences plus an inventory of all the cattle that were being moved. I posted one by special delivery to Scotland, to get to Gordon early the next day; we would keep one ourselves, and each driver would have a pack. I also put together eight packed lunches with drinks, because the stipulation with the movement licence was that no wagon would stop on the journey.

By nine o'clock on Thursday evening our farm drive was a solid line of parked lorries. I served a stew supper for all the men, then we all bedded down for an early night—the lorry drivers in their wagons.

John woke at 2.30 and got up and started milking at 3 a.m. Charlie and the other farm workers arrived very early, and even the DEFRA representative got to the farm at 5 a.m., which is when I started cooking breakfast for the drivers.

As the cows were milked John wanted them to be loaded, and as each wagon filled up they would set off individually.

'No,' said the Ministry inspector. 'They should all wait and go together.'

John felt this was terribly wrong, as the cows would be stressed by having to stand in the wagons too long. 'No, no, no! You're not making my cows wait like that,' insisted John. 'They go immediately they're loaded. I will not accept any other way.'

I could see that if these two men came to verbal blows there would be great difficulties, so I decided to be the go-between, talking to one, then running over to the other, mostly trying to persuade the DEFRA man to do it John's way. Eventually he agreed.

So at 7 a.m. the first wagon got on the road and started the long journey up north. John put the last cow on to the last wagon two hours later, then ran into the house to have a quick shower and get changed. I'd put our suitcase in the car, and as soon as John got in I started the drive to Scotland. John was so stressed and emotional that he couldn't have driven anywhere. We quickly caught up with the last wagon and over the next few hours passed the next one, and the next one, on the long journey up the motorway. Although we had never been to the farm in Scotland before, we knew exactly where it was as we had had such good directions from Gordon.

'Put your foot down,' commanded John. Then, after one rather risky piece of overtaking, he exclaimed, 'Bloody hell, woman! Are you trying to kill me?'

As we drove down Gordon and Fiona's farm drive we could see in front of us the first wagon, which had only just arrived. Gordon and his sons were washing down the exterior with power hoses and disinfectant.

Then it was our turn to be power hosed. John jumped out and was there to see them open up the back doors of that first lorry. He had seen all his cows on to each wagon, and now it seemed he would be able to get all his cows off each lorry at the other end. He inspected the animals coming down the lorry ramps, as did the DEFRA inspector who had also just arrived in his own car. The cows were then ushered into a nearby small field and all seemed to be well. John was visibly very pleased. Immediately other lorries started arriving, and for a while we had a conveyor belt of lorries being power hosed, then cows taken off, inspected by John and the official, and going straight into the field.

John was so elated that he had been able personally to supervise all his cows on to the wagons at one end and see them all off and into the field at the other. We were all so pleased, too, when we realised that not a single one of them had sustained any injuries. You would expect by the law of averages that one would have trodden on another or lain down on her neighbour, but none had.

They did, of course, seem quite shocked after the journey, but when they were all mixed up together they behaved as one herd again, and went up and smelt and nudged their best pals. There

211

was no fighting for position, as is normally the case when unfamiliar cows are put together. They knew each other, and just fitted together as the original herd. Then we humans all went and had a cup of tea in the farmhouse and at last relaxed a little, although John and I and Fiona and Gordon did not at the time appreciate how dreadfully stressed we had all become because of the difficulties in facilitating this move.

Very soon it was time for milking, and it was decided that John and Gordon would do this first one through the new milking parlour together. Milking cows through a new parlour is notoriously difficult until they get used to the different regime. However, that afternoon it was amazingly easy. John went out and called the cows as he would normally do, and because they immediately recognised his voice I suppose they felt calmer and more at home. Steadily they just filed into the parlour, and with little trouble were milked by him and Gordon.

Fiona and I were in the house when the two men came back in. The last few months had been so nerve-racking, and the disaster that Fiona and Gordon had gone through with foot and mouth so traumatic. But the expressions on the two men's faces as they walked through the door that night were like those of conquering heroes. Together they had accomplished this feat, and although they had been strangers when they met five months previously they were certainly the best of friends now.

After supper that evening Gordon and Fiona paid us the balance of the money for the purchase of the herd and shook hands on a good deal done.

I don't think any of us had slept properly for several nights, and as we got into bed in their guest bedroom we realised how the last few days had taken their toll. Although we were dog-tired we couldn't sleep peacefully, but tossed and turned fretfully for most of the night. I understand that Gordon sat staring out of his bedroom window for several hours, unable to believe that once again, after the agonies they had gone through, they had dairy cows on their farm.

John was up early the next day to milk with Gordon. He called the cows through the new parlour as usual, but this time with Gordon doing more of the jobs and slowly getting them used to him. By that afternoon the reaction to the last few days had caught up with us all, so we went to our respective bedrooms and had a nap for a few hours—something I'd never seen John do, and I believe was also alien to our Scottish friends.

Next day the men saw that the cows weren't drinking from their water source, a wide river which flowed through the whole farm. We wondered why, then realised that the cows had never seen a river before and therefore didn't know what to do with it. Some time was spent cajoling them to dip their toes in the water and drink, which they eventually did.

John spent the next few days between milkings getting Gordon conversant with all the dairy records that had been brought up in our car. Ours had been a closed herd, in that we had bred all our own stock for the past forty years. Only pedigree bulls had been used, so the records were quite important.

On the last two days John stopped milking and

put all the records on to Gordon and Fiona's new computer system. By the 10th of September John decided it was time to leave. Gordon had gradually taken over milking the cows, who seemed content and settled, gradually getting used to him and his two sons. We were very impressed by how well they ran the farm: they obviously cared deeply for the welfare of all their animals, and no expense was spared in providing the best for them in every way.

After breakfast the next day we all lined up for photographs. A few tears were shed—though they were tears of relief at how well this transition had all gone and tears of joy at having made such good new friends. John walked out into the fields by himself where the cows were grazing, and slowly walked round them all. We all silently watched him from the house. This was a once-in-a-lifetime event, and we could see how upset he was. He had looked after this herd since he was fifteen years old. He had bred their grandmothers and great-grandmothers and knew their ancestry intimately. He still knew each of their two hundred-plus names: Agatha, Annabel, Beatrice, Beth, Delores, Ethel, Nancy, Susan, Samantha . . . and he said his own goodbyes.

As he returned to the house he wept openly, and we didn't really know what to say to him because we all knew that nothing would alleviate the great loss he felt. Gordon kept saying that we were welcome to come back and inspect the cows at any time. John could drive up to Scotland and do a milking whenever he wanted. We knew this offer was made with complete sincerity. 'Come and have a holiday with us in a few months,' they said. Then Gordon started to get upset when describing the wonderful friendship John and he had made. I knew this couldn't go on. We'd all said what we wanted to say, so I just took matters in hand and said, 'It's time for us to go.' I got into the driving seat of the car, and quickly we set off.

We know we couldn't have devised any better way for our cows to go out of our hands. They were kept together as a herd, and their new owners were the best and most conscientious farmers imaginable. They cared deeply for their stock and kept them in pristine condition, and we had been told we could come back and see them any time. John knew it was the right decision to make, but his sentiments for his cows had been developed over four decades and that goes deep for the good man that he is.

I just drove that morning, and wasn't too sure where we would end up. In the afternoon we eventually found ourselves in the Balmoral area and booked into a hotel just a few miles away. As soon as we had checked into our room we decided to go into the little town to buy a couple of books for bedtime reading. Amazingly, there choosing a book was a lady whom we knew from down in Derbyshire. We had a pleasant chat and then said our goodbyes, as we wanted to go and find a nice spot on the banks of the Spey. John was feeling better, but we felt we just wanted to find somewhere quiet and enjoy the beautiful scenery.

When we had parked I thought I would telephone Marjorie, my secretary, for the lady we'd met by chance in the bookshop was her cousin. I thought she'd find the coincidence amazing.

'Oh, Pat, put your car radio on,' she said. 'The most awful thing has happened!'

And there, watching the beautiful River Spey with the magnificent scenery surrounding it, John put the car radio on and caught the news. Yes, the news from New York on 11 September 2001 put the feelings of sadness we'd had that day into complete perspective. We decided it was impossible to sit there and feel contented in such picturesque surroundings, so we went back to the hotel and viewed the dreadful scenes on the television in our room. As we walked out on to our small balcony, below us we heard a group of Americans talking and realised that their world would never be the same again.

Our holiday in Scotland came to an end. Gradually we wound our way through the lowlands and over the border into England. I think, given the choice, we would willingly have stayed away forever, for a world without dairy cows would be so new to us.

We were met by Ben, Sarah and Charlie, who actually seemed pleased to see us back. Amazingly, the house was immaculate—always a suspicious sign. How many illicit parties had they had? Charlie had been in charge of the children! But never mind: nothing was broken or marked, so whatever they had been up to I didn't really want to know.

The Bureau office had been looked after by Marjorie, and with a quick scan over things I could see she had done a superb job. But messages had been left to ring George from the Forest of Dean and Gordon in the Falkland Islands, and she felt that as I knew these men well, I should telephone them myself.

George had been introduced to Nancy in the

early spring and they were the oldest clients on my register. I remembered I'd said, 'An alliance such as this would be a miracle' when I first introduced them, because adapting your lifestyle is more difficult the older you get. And it's more difficult than ever when you live four hours apart, as I knew they did.

The most extreme in terms of distance of my current introductions were Gordon in the Falklands and Jane who lived in Wales. *I wonder how things are going for him*, I thought, as I looked at the Falklands time chart I'd made about twenty years ago when men from there first started to approach the Bureau. *Yes, there's a chance he'll be in the farmhouse*, I thought as I dialled the number.

Instantly a female voice answered. I'm always very careful if this happens when I'm phoning a man who usually lives alone, and wary of what I say. Immediately I asked to speak to Gordon. There was a short silence, then this voice shouted, 'Is it Pat? I recognise your voice. It's Pat, isn't it?'

Tentatively I said, 'Yes, yes it is.'

'Well, this is Jane,' she shouted. 'I'm here and it's wonderful.'

'Oh, Jane! Jane, how lovely,' I said. I was so excited, then Jane started talking very quickly and loudly as if she was shouting right across the Atlantic. But she just wanted to tell me all about her and Gordon.

'He's a great man,' she said. 'The community's lovely and everyone's so friendly. The farm's very isolated and not many people live close by, but that's how I like it. It's an outdoor life, which I love—and Gordon's so good with his horses.' Then she added, 'He's here now, and he wants to talk to you.'

'Hello, Pat. I just wanted to say thank you, thank you, thank you so much for putting Jane into my life. I know I have a wonderful future ahead now, and we can't thank you enough. I thought it was an impossible task, so many thousands of miles away from Britain. Already we've got plans for our future together. Jane will have to go back to the UK for a while, but she'll be giving up her job and house soon after to come back here. To be with me!'

As I put the phone down I spontaneously threw both arms high in the air, as I usually do after I've heard about a successful matchmaking, and shouted with absolute joy, 'Yes, yes, that's great!'

The next call I'd been asked to make was to George, always very courteous and proper in addressing me.

'I have to say, Mrs Warren, Nancy and I have truly fallen in love. I thought I would meet someone just for companionship at my age. But, no—Nancy and I felt there was something very special and strong between us right from the start. We're now looking at properties not far from her, and as soon as we see a home we both like we'll be putting our two houses up for sale and getting married. I feel so in love with her, and I know she feels the same. We want to enjoy every moment we have, because as we're both in our eighties our time together may not be too long.'

The call was ended by George going completely out of character and showing very obvious emotion. He wept a little over the phone, and between the tears of joy he said, 'Thank you for helping me find this very special love with Nancy that I thought would never happen again at my age.'

As I put the telephone down I too nearly shed a little tear for the wonderful happiness they had found. *Pat, don't be so silly*, I said to myself. *You've had good news like this before, from different couples, literally hundreds of times since you started the Bureau.* But I know that no matter how many times I receive such good news, I cannot help being touched by it.

A lot had happened that day in September. We'd arrived home from Scotland, and it was lovely to see the children and be back at the farmhouse. I'd dealt with Bureau phone calls and received wonderful news that had completely changed the lives of those involved. The farm definitely seemed different. For forty years, twice a day, our cows had walked past us to their milking rendezvous, but now everywhere seemed so silent and you could listen to this strange quietness and feel the slower pace of life. *But then this is what we wanted*, I said to myself, *and what was planned for*, and I reminded myself that we had actually achieved our goal.

John and I walked out into the fields that evening. There was a glorious sunset that sent brilliant shafts of warm light over the farmland. The beauty of the surrounding countryside in this honeyed light made us realise that we had come to a moment of change in our life, just as change is happening all the time in nature. And we knew that 'to every thing there is a season, and a time to every purpose under the heaven.'

CHIVERS LARGE PRINT –direct–

If you have enjoyed this Large Print book and would like to build up your own collection of Large Print books, please contact

Chivers Large Print Direct

Chivers Large Print Direct offers you a full service:

• Prompt mail order service

• Easy-to-read type

• The very best authors

• Special low prices

For further details either call Customer Services on (01225) 336552 or write to us at Chivers Large Print Direct, **FREEPOST**, Bath BA1 3ZZ

Telephone Orders: **FREEPHONE** 08081 72 74 75